Disclaimer:

The author of this book has tried to present the most accurate information to his knowledge at the time of writing. This book is intended for information purposes only. The author does not imply any results to those using this book, nor are they responsible for any results brought about by the usage of the information contained herein.

No part of this book may be reprinted, electronically transmitted or reproduced in any format without the express written permission of the author.

Welcome

If you have stopped to read this book then I guess you are having some fun and games with your MRP / ERP system. For ease in this guide I will use the terms MRP (Materials Requirements Planning), MRP II (Manufacturing Resources Planning) and ERP (Enterprise Resources Planning) as being interchangeable. Although they are not precisely the same things, this book is fundamentally going to look at how you get the core elements of an MRP system working properly. These elements are common in most modern systems, whether the vendor describes it as MRP / MRPII / ERP. The fundamental design of these systems is the same under the bonnet.

Are you struggling with any of the following?
- Bloated order books and late deliveries
- Materials not being ordered on time
- Being stuck between 'going Lean' and using MRP
- Spreadsheets being used instead of the system
- A general lack of understanding about how the system works
- Conflict with other departments, leading to poor information
- Fire fighting due to errors made by following the current system
- Confusion, irritation and a feeling of running around like

'headless chickens'

The above list is made up of comments I hear from clients. This book aims to address these issues in a logical approach. Each section of the book builds upon the previous section until you have created your own improvement plan to take your business forward.

Most systems are generic once you get under the facade of the interfaces. They all run from a set of rules and this book is going to look at some of the common issues I see businesses struggling with when it comes to running MRP systems effectively. This book doesn't aim to be an exhaustive discourse on the subject, more of a practical set of tools, a Pareto of issues if you like.

I spend a fair bit of my working life helping businesses to find out why they aren't getting the results they want from their MRP system and one common factor I have noticed is that the system doesn't get fully configured by the time implementation goes live. When that happens, whoosh, we're off in to the thick of busy working and we never go back to sort it out. Roll forward a year or two and no one can remember what needs to be configured, or how. Even worse, poor working habits may have sunk in and workarounds may have emerged as the normal way of working. Add in the factor of people moving on from their jobs, bringing with it degradation in overall knowledge about your MRP system, and you end up in a downward spiral.

I tend to think of MRP system user's attitude to their system as being a bit like when people are sceptical of Sat Nav systems in their cars. We know that the Sat Nav has the map. We know that it has been programmed with our information. We know that it has got us to our destination in the past, but we are still unsure of the route it offers us, and so we take 'educated' deviations along the course only to find out that the Sat Nav knew a really good route all along. Admittedly some of my early experiences with Sat Navs were sketchy, but largely my problems have been with entering the wrong post code into the destination field of the Sat Nav. There is a parallel with MRP systems. We don't configure them properly (whether from a system point of view or from a component level) and then spend our lives fighting the information they give back to us.

I'm not suggesting that we configure the system and then blindly accept the information as the gospel. I think we should still review the information and consider its validity periodically, but what I hope you get out of this book is some ideas or answers as to how you can resolve the current issues with your MRP system and then find a better way of working with it. Instead of wrestling with the information and deciding to do something different I hope that you take the opportunity to stop, reflect and then change the rules in your system so that it gives you information in the way that you want it, in a way that helps your business, without additional interpretation.

This book exists because I wanted there to be a practical guide that was short enough to be read and useful enough to help, which could make a difference to MRP systems and their performance within the business. There are many really good, world class, examples of MRP systems in use and there are myriads more of ones that aren't so good. Some of the poorer implementations reflect the text of the MRP books written in the late 1970s and 1980s about MRP introduction. The organisational problems are the same, the training issues are the same, the lack of proper use is the same, and it goes on. At the time of writing (2013), I sometimes feel like the general usage of these systems hasn't progressed to where it should be. I hope that this book will help to close out some of these gaps and we are able to gain the performance and profitability for our businesses that MRP systems should help us to achieve.

Table of Contents

This book is split into five sections.

In a little more detail, the main sections cover:

Section One – Your Starting Point

The first section will look at some of the fundamentals of MRP decision making and a couple of points to get you started on your journey.

Section Two - System Rules: Key Factors In Making MRP Work

The second section looks at the basic rules MRP systems work from. I know that MRP systems can vary, but they are basically a database and an interface. I won't assume that I can fix every different MRP type of problem just because I have used a wide range of them over the years, but I will give you a good place to go and find answers to your issues.

Section Three - Using It Properly

Section three then discusses ways of using your MRP system. In particular I will look at the type of business approach that makes using your MRP system easier and more consistent.

Section Four – Making Further Progress

In section four, I will look at a number of activities that can take your MRP system's performance forward, moving your business towards its objectives.

Section Five - Action Planning

Finally, in section five, I share some of my general views about managing improvement projects and continuous improvement. These ideas can apply to any kind of continuous improvement / change management approach also.

So, if you're ready to get started, let's go.

Section One –Your Starting Point

MRP systems are a collection of parts. You have databases, interfaces, rules and information. If you peel away the skin of a system, that's pretty much all you have to play with. The interesting ingredient to add to this recipe is the people who use this system.

This section of the book looks at some of the immediate issues, and background considerations to getting the most out of your MRP system. They may seem to be preparatory and they are. In many businesses that I have attended to however, these items were not developed and so I include them at the start of this book to give you a chance to make sure that you have not missed them out also.

Although the bulk of the improvements to your system will come from the later sections, making sure that these elements are correct is an essential place to start.

How Do You Want Your Business To Run?

Knowing how you want your business to operate is the first place we must start if we want to ensure that the way that we have set up our system is going to serve our purposes. There are fundamentally three approaches to setting up an MRP system. They are Engineer To Order (ETO), Make To Order (MTO) and Make To Stock (MTS).

ETO businesses make new products each time they take an order on, unless it is a repeat order of course. Each product could include new components or use a combination of existing components to fulfil the design and this extra work at the front end will affect the lead times of the products you manufacture. Any business that makes something for the first time will experience the ETO approach but it is what you plan to do next with the products that will determine if you need to look at the approach differently.

The next approach, which leads on from the ETO approach is the Make To Order method. This is where you sell repeated items without necessarily going through the design and engineering steps that you would have done the first time you created the product. Whereas the ETO approach would look to minimise the stock levels and purchase materials on demand, the make to order approach may require better arrangements to be made with suppliers, or even consider a degree of stock holding to maintain supply lead times.

This then takes us to the final main approach, Make To Stock. The MTS approach drives the production element of your business to regulate a stock level that you have told your system to maintain. If you have certain products that you have demand for and you want to ensure the supply of these products then using a stock level (buffer) could be a viable option to help your MRP system plan your production.

As with most businesses you may need to blend the three approaches to get the results you want. For example, if you are following a mass customisation approach then base products may be stocked and then the final items are produced on a MTO basis. Certain products may be better suited to MTO and some will always be engineered upon request.

The reason for including this information at the start of the book is to make sure that you know the difference between the types as this will affect how you configure components within MRP later on. Getting the right combination of approaches is essential for your business' ability to deliver and will reduce the complexity of managing your organisation.

The final item that I would like to cover here is that of families. One of the stumbling blocks that I see on a regular basis is when businesses see every product as being different, particularly when it comes to a strong ETO environment. When each product that enters the order book is requiring some form of design work people can become despondent about the MRP approach. It can seem like there is a lot of work to do to update and maintain a system of this nature, but there is a simple way to approach this. Often products can be grouped into families. This can be based on size, machining requirements, assembly method, or whatever makes logical sense. When you are able to create groups, or families, then you can apply slightly more generic information to your MRP system. This can lead to a slight degrading to the accuracy of the system but it can also give you the speed and simplicity that makes the whole system work better overall.

The families approach has been criticised in some quarters for the inaccuracy that it can bring with it. My objective in this book is to share some ideas with you that can make your MRP system work for your business and help you to achieve the results you want. Being pragmatic about some aspects of the system configuration can bring these results quicker for the sake of a few percentage points of accuracy. If you are wondering about this small loss then I would challenge you about the current accuracy of the information that you are working with. I would rather see MRP working with a lower degree of accuracy, but with the right performance outputs. This is often better than a system that is underutilised with the business struggling along, juggling all of the requirements placed upon it.

So, confirm to yourself how you want your business to work and let's move on to the next preparatory item.

Action Step

- Decide what type of approach would serve your business best; ETO, MTO, MTS, or a combination of these.

Where Are You On Your Journey?

Implementing systems can take time. The amount of time you need is dependent on a number of factors. One of the biggest factors is where your team is in relation to their understanding and usage of systems. Some businesses try to get their teams to accelerate the implementation of systems, including MRP, because the sooner it gets implemented the sooner the benefits should be realised.

I agree with the notion of sooner is better than later, but if the pace doesn't match the education and support (let alone leadership) in the use of a system then the results may be less than stunning. It needs to be recognised that just because you are ready for the change doesn't mean that your team is. Determining where the team is and what the gap is between that position and one where the team is fully engaged and prepared to operate an MRP system is the job of a leader. Where is your team with regards to this journey?

How many systems have you had to date? Have you implemented other systems into your business but so far not witnessed the impact it should have. If this resonates with you then you are not alone. There are many businesses that have implemented new systems and instead of improving the efficiency of the business it appears to have merely increased the level of administrative staff employed by the business. Has this happened to you?

One of the telltale signs that something isn't quite working is when you see new faces appearing in a production control team, or similar support departments. Additional people who are responsible for the administrative work that was originally expected to be handled by the new system should raise the warning flag. If that is something that you recognise then it is time to ask yourself some questions about your approach to implementing systems. The later sections of this book will help you with the configuration considerations you need to undertake. The disciplines and routines that you need to develop is something that I will discuss later on. There is of course more to leading your team than this, and it is a challenge outside of the scope of this book. However, I hope that if you are responsible for leading your team through the change process then you will be able to feel more confident after reading this book.

Systems can take time to implement, and more importantly, embed. Using the ideas in this book to create your own improvement plan should seem straightforward by the time you reach the end of this book. Keeping the focus within the team to achieve the results is always easier when you feel comfortable about what changes to make.

Have you had other systems working in your business? What

was different about these systems, and what was different about the way that you approached the implementation? If you can answer these questions you will probably find some good ideas to help you improve the current standing of your MRP system. Some businesses find that the systems that worked more effectively were smaller and that they found the whole process of implementing the system easier. This made making it a part of their day to day business a far more simple and manageable process. If this is your experience then take each section of this book step by step. Using this bite size approach can make a big change project seem a lot simpler and a lot more achievable. Allow your team members to get onboard with the changes as easily as possible.

Knowing where your team is and your past history with implementing systems can help you to make better informed decisions about how you want to tackle the improvements required by your system. Like a farm, you need to plant the seeds first, then water and nurture them before you can harvest the crops. You can't jump the sequence. Implementing and embedding an effective system needs you to know your own sequence of activities and then to follow them in order. What are the steps they need to take in order to compound their learning and 'be in the right place'?

Now, let's move on to the next issue – finding where we ignore our current system.

Action Steps

- Find out how 'receptive' your team is. Where do they need to be in order to fully adopt and embed an MRP system?

- Find your past successes. What were the common factors? What can you use with your MRP system?

Workarounds And Underutilised Modules

A tell tale sign that your system isn't fully understood, or embedded, is that of workarounds. Workarounds are alternative, non-system methods that are used in the business instead of embracing the functionality of the system. Granted sometimes the system will not do exactly what you want it to do, but the risk with workarounds is that you are introducing a new set of data to your business. Another set of data means more management and potential conflicts. This does not help you simplify your business practices and improve. As mentioned in the previous section, workarounds can also increase your head count as well as providing other management issues.

A common method of creating a workaround is to dump the data from the system into a spreadsheet. The flexibility of spreadsheets makes them an obvious choice, and many people are familiar with (basic) spreadsheet commands. One of my gripes with using workarounds like a spreadsheet is that the data flow is usually one way. This means that whatever is done in the spreadsheet never makes its way back into the system. This means that the MRP system never benefits from the updated information and therefore cannot give you an output that you can work with. You become tied to the spreadsheet and build dependency on both the document itself and the person that created it. Very rarely do these workarounds get formalised and so you put your business at risk from an operations management point of view.

Another sign you can look out for is the level of unused modules in your MRP system. Most MRP systems are comprised of a series of interlinked modules (such as Sales Order Processing, Purchasing, Works Orders etc...) and when you have a specific module not being used then you will usually find that this is because there is a lack of understanding within the organisation about how it works. Quite often the module will fill the perceived gap in functionality, but perhaps it isn't understood fully and is hence ignored. Clarifying the purpose and functionality of the modules contained in your system can be a worthwhile exercise. If there are clear gaps in the utilisation of the system then there could be an opportunity to remove workarounds.

An excessive list of bespoke system reports being available can indicate a lack of understanding around the functionality of the MRP system. Most modern systems provide on screen reporting as well as standard reports to help users decipher the data contained in the system. I have seen a correlation between businesses who don't understand their systems and the volume of reports they have available. As time progresses and the acceptance of the system improve I also see the rationalisation of reports. Although this might not be the case in your business I have seen it too many times to dismiss this 'cause and effect' relationship. I will revisit the issue of reports near the end of this book.

I suggest that you use the three points above (spreadsheets, unused modules and excessive reports) as a dipstick for your own business. Have a look at what is currently happening in your business and determine how much of the system is being used the way it should. Even with a good system selection procedure at the outset I still see these feral ways of working creep back into a system's operation. Knowing where you are will help you to create a suitable action plan later on.

Action Steps

- Find the workarounds that 'support' your system. Work out why they exist, close the gaps in knowledge, learning etc... and eliminate them one by one.

- Look for redundancy in your MRP modules. Find out what they are for and identify opportunities to further remove workarounds or increase the functionality of your system.

Know Your Demo System

Over the years I have met many people who 'fear the system'. They fear making a mistake with the setting up of components, changing the configuration of the system or when using utilities programs contained within the system. Whereas a paper based system can hide mistakes and problems for days and weeks, your MRP system will not be as kind. An incorrectly configured part of your system will probably wreak havoc moments after you run your MRP cycle. Purchase orders and works orders can radically shift after changing small details within the setup of your system. There is a good approach, however, that you can take to prevent this 'fear' from stopping you make the most of your system.

Many businesses have access to a 'demo' system. This is often the same system but one that points to a different set of data, allowing you to play with the information without consequence. Making the demo system your friend can allow you to explore the functionality of the system and try out the various elements. You can try to break the system but can remain safe in the knowledge that you aren't going to adversely affect the business whilst doing so.

Using a demo system is a great way to gain real learning experience. Whilst I advocate Standard Operating Procedures (SOPs) there is something essential about being able to press those buttons and pull those levers in order to go through the practical procedures to gain experience. If there is no SOP written and you need to change your system then you may need to try other MRP options. Playing with the system in a safe environment is a good way to experiment with the ideas contained in this book.

Having access to real data is also important as it can give you the right feel when you are playing with the system. Many businesses that I know have arranged with their IT department to copy across the live database information once a month (or more often). This provides a meaningful experience to the users who want to play in their test areas. Many MRP software companies can provide test data, but if it looks nothing like your real data then the trials may be sub-optimal. If your Bills of Materials are multi level and your test data is relatively flat, for example, then you may find that your experiments lack the substance you want.

I mentioned above the opportunity to try and 'break' the system. In the demo version of the system you can try and work out what the limits of your system are. When I say 'break' I am referring to your understanding of the constraints of the system improving. Can it process your information in a certain way? Can it handle specific types of configuration in your components? If you have a question and you can configure your system to accept the change you can test it. If the test goes wrong when you operate the system then you will know how the system reacts and can avoid doing that on the real system. From doing this kind of experiment you can gain insights into how you can further improve your system.

Going back to SOPs for a moment, the demo system is a good place to write these instructional guides. The data is real (although out of date) so any screenshots you choose to use in the document will look authentic. The demo system becomes really useful for doing this when you want to capture the MRP run, or similar programs, mid cycle for a screenshot. This prevents you from disturbing other system users, or affecting the data in the system. Using the demo system can allow you to write your SOPs, recording the most sensitive of activities, without bothering other users.

Making the demo system your friend can allow you to get more out of your system in the long run. You can use it to test your ideas and see what works for you. If there are elements of this book later on that make you want to reconfigure the system then try it in the demo system first. Understanding exactly what the output is on your system with your data is only something that you can do; using the demo system makes this a safe encounter. So, find where your demo system lives and see if you can make it your ally.

Action Steps

- Find your demo system.

- Use it to test out configuration options and ideas you have for improving how your system works.

- Gain confidence by testing out options and theories in a safe environment.

Understand The Linkages

As with all systems, processes within MRP systems need to flow together. The information in one part of the system often finds its way into another part of the system. The data might not necessarily move, but it may be converted into some other form of data (like hours being converted into a monetary value). When there is a lack of appreciation about the need for good data in other parts of the MRP system bad practices can develop and this is often where I see the problem lying. If we get better acquainted with what happens to our data once it leaves us then we may choose to do something different.

Appreciating that there is a flow of data is probably the best place to start. Sharing with all the teams how the data flows from one part of the MRP system to the next can give some people a wakeup call. I have witnessed many companies who have witnessed a decrease in data quality over time because the importance of the information in the business is not clear. When times get busy and the capacity versus quality debate rears its head then we risk our methods of working being shortened in order to keep up with the workload. If there are no apparent consequences then the new method may become the standard and over time this shortcut can affect the other parts of your business.

Clarifying the data requirements of other departments in your business can help to sort out these issues. Knowing what other departments do with your data, when they need and how they need it can be all it takes to start experiencing better information. Putting the needs of other departments into context can be a short process to undertake, a simple spider diagram relating all of your internal data customers can often do the trick.

If you have variation in your data entries into the MRP system, such as a text field in a notes box, then standardising the way that you enter your data could be worth considering. When people who use this information have to think and decipher the messages then quite often the information stops getting looked at. If the data is ignored then the process can then start to break down because 'why bother?' Although I have already touched on downward spirals with MRP systems, it is worth emphasising that poor quality and inconsistent data accelerates the process. Good standardised data on the other hand helps to engage users with the system and help to maintain a good discipline around the use of the system. So, if you have room for variation in your data entries, consider developing a fixed / standard format for writing these messages.

Like most of the topics in this book, getting the right people from the right teams to have a conversation about how their parts of the system work and their requirements for data can be a quick, low cost and simple method to get the fixes made. As I have implied in this section, most of the declines in data quality are due to a lack of understanding rather than a malicious attempt to cut corners with the quality of the data in the system. Developing ways to detect poor data quality is a topic we'll cover later in the book, but often it only comes to light when someone interrogates the information and finds that they cannot use the data in a meaningful way. This retrospective review isn't the way forward and won't help your business. Managing data quality is not an impossible task as we will discuss later on.

Action Steps

- Find where your data is poor.
- Find the person / people responsible and educate them on why the data needs to be right.
- Answer their questions and help them to develop better ways of working.

Importing And Exporting

When we are improving the information in our systems we can find ourselves with a rather laborious and time consuming task ahead of us. The amount of data entry that we can be faced with can be huge and, although we can rope in our colleagues, the size of the task could have a detrimental effect on the rest of the business. Thankfully should this situation arise then most modern MRP systems have excellent importing and exporting functionality that (like the demo system) you would be well advised to become friends with.

From the point of view of checking information, it can be painstaking to review individual records within your system. Getting the whole lot dumped into a spreadsheet can allow you to quickly manipulate data to check for specific patterns of information that may be incorrect, or segment the data so visual inspection of records can be done a lot faster. Whilst report writers are good for making this happen too, when an export comes from the MRP system you know it will be in the right format to re-insert (or import) the data back into the database at a later date in time. I have seen many businesses spend a lot of hours trying to comb through records manually over a period of weeks where the whole task could be completed in less than half an hour via a download from the system.

Once you have the data out of the system you can use your

spreadsheet abilities to quickly sort and amend data before importing back into the system. Whilst I don't advocate general workarounds surrounding MRP systems I do support the use of external tools to help with a quick turnaround of data in remedial situations. If you are familiar with the Pareto principle (or 80/20 principle) you will know that a few inputs can give you a large output in a given system. Exporting and quickly manipulating data before amending it and importing it back into a system is a very efficient use of time. Instead of having to slog your guts out doing the work you can do in minutes what might take days or weeks.

Extending the idea of using spreadsheets to manipulate the data is the idea of using codes within your products / components to make this manipulation easier. When you export data from your system to a spreadsheet you will need to find something within the data to allow you to sort the information. When you set products up in your system you usually get options to include various codes, or classes, to distinguish product types, or raw material types, or whatever you include in your system. When you export data you can use these codes to help navigate your way around your data. If you haven't got such codes then you may find that you will have to be more creative with your searching techniques, which can make the process longer and more risky (in the sense that you omit data during your searches). If you don't have such codes in your system then you could use the exporting and importing function to put these codes in place.

Exporting and importing of data is an important remedial technique. You shouldn't need to do it too often but, when you do, it can save you a lot of time.

Action Steps

- Find out how to export and import data within your MRP system.

- Set up identification / class codes to distinguish different types of parts.

- Use the Pareto principle to quickly identify parts that need configuring and use the export / import function to make changes quickly.

Case Studies

To help put these points into context I thought I would share a couple of anonymous case studies.

The first case study is of an established manufacturing business that makes components for aircraft. Although they had been MRPII users for over two decades, prior to the latest system being introduced, the previous systems had never been fully established. As a result of the systems never truly operating in the way that they were designed, people developed workarounds. The lack of credible data in the system meant that the people downstream couldn't use their system properly and led to them having to create their own workarounds too.

This mentality of not using the system flowed into the latest system they had implemented and although the ability to interrogate the system was vastly improved (along with the speed of the system working) the users failed to change their habits pre-implementation. When I worked with them they were fighting their information and still trying to do things long hand.

The configuration of their system led to frustrating phone calls with the software's support team, so we used the demo version of the system and determined accurately how the system was operating using their information. This allowed us to define the choices we needed to make, plus the options that were available to us. Using the demo system also allowed us to work with the users to test out the correct ways of working in an environment where it didn't matter if things went wrong. Things didn't go wrong and the users gained significant confidence with the system.

The level of fighting with the system (in terms of trying to override the system's advice and recommendations) diminished too, allowing the users to spend more time on doing the important things and less time administrating the system itself. By refining the routines that the team worked to and re-engineering a couple of the internal processes we were able to drop eight work days of administration from the team's monthly workload. You can imagine what this did for the team's morale as well as their ability to work on the right tasks.

This business' performance improved directly as a result. Incoming material supplies improved, stocks reduced, scheduling accuracy improved, on time delivery improved and there was a dramatic reduction in customer queries bombarding the customer support team!

The second case study I want to share with you is about another manufacturing company, this time producing bespoke components for the power generation sector. Their system was introduced three years prior to my involvement with the business, and like the previous example their company had experienced many years of MRP systems prior to this system's introduction.

Whilst in this example there were not as many workarounds in operation, the sheer volume of effort it took to maintain the system was huge. Each product was designed for each order; there were very few repeat orders. For each order on the MRP system there was a large amount of effort involved in preparing the shop floor paperwork and also in the purchasing and designing activities.

Standing back from the busy work it became clear that generic families could be used to drop the volume of work required at the shop floor paperwork stage from half of an engineer's time to five minutes per day. This saved time was then re-directed to production line improvement work.

The shop floor data capture modules weren't being used; they had never been switched on, let alone adopted. The shop floor teams wanted better information as it took a full time job to merely keep a list approximately up to date. The teams wanted immediate information and the manual system wasn't coping. So, the teams decided to embrace the shop floor data capture information and this freed up the original planning role for improving the front end loading issues into the business.

These two changes made a significant difference to the operational performance of the business. The lead time dropped from nearly twenty weeks to under four and on time delivery performance rose from 22% to a peak of 98% (settling at a 95% average) over the same period.

The system didn't change, the team did. A few minor modifications to the approach they took with their system allowed for some large benefits to be gained.

Both of these examples aren't unusual. If you keep reading and applying the ideas from the later sections in this book then you too will be able to make significant improvements to how your MRP system serves your business. Thankfully the changes aren't too technical either, more managerial. The people with the technical skills have already done their bit – they built your MRP system. The trick is for you to now use the system to its full effect.

Summary

This section of the book is all about the top level management of your approach to using MRP systems within your business. I'll get onto the more technical aspects of setting up / modifying your system later on, but don't worry – it won't get too deep. Before you move on however I want to recap on what we have covered so far.

We started off by reviewing the type of business that you wish to operate. The main choices are Engineer to Order (ETO), Make to Order (MTO) and Make to Stock (MTS). Choosing the most appropriate option can help you to think through how you want to operate your system and the management of your teams.

Your place on the journey is important when trying to take your team with you. Knowing how quickly they can progress and how slowly you need to take the improvement work can help to circumvent problems with the changes you want to make. Don't try to rush the improvements, but do your best to accelerate the progress being made.

Workarounds can derail systems and if you can spot them in your organisation then please do your best to find out why the system isn't being adhered to. Getting to the root cause of why the workarounds exist is vital for making longer term gains with your MRP system.

The demo system that lurks in your business can be an absolute God-send when you want to get your team to try out their ideas and to find out how your system actually works. This element goes hand in hand with the workarounds as better knowledge of the system can help to eliminate these additional methods of working.

Information flows between departments work via MRP systems and gaining a better understanding of these can also help to improve the uptake of the system as it stands. Lack of understanding can be a real killer to properly utilising the system and, as you know; better information can lead to better business decisions and better performance.

Importing and exporting data from your system can make modifications to the data a fast and palatable option. Making the changes 'long hand' by changing each individual record can be soul destroying as well as time consuming and is prone to errors. Finding out how your systems deal with imported and exported data can save you a lot of time should you find that your current set up of the system (or the components within the system) needs to be altered.

In the next section we are going to look at the more technical elements of configuring your MRP system so that it works the way that you want it to work.

Section Two - System Rules (Key Factors In Making MRP Work)

Although there are many elements within an MRP system that can be altered and adjusted, there are only a few different components that make major differences to how the system operates. This section of the book looks at these foundations and how adjusting them can make your life easier.

During my travels I have seen a good number of systems that have these elements set up in a way that doesn't help the business. The system tries to 'over rule' the user at every turn, but that is not the way it should be. If the system is not set up correctly in the first place it cannot behave in the way that the user wants or expects. This ongoing fight leads to many of the workaround issues that we have touched upon in the first section of this book.

Correct configuration can be done quickly and effectively. The aim of this section is to help you to do this and start getting some real benefits out of your system.

Lead Times

The lead times that you hold in your system can make a big difference to the way that your system behaves. There also appears to be a great deal of confusion with lead times generally. As you may already know there is not just one lead time for the business.

Depending on how your business is defined (Engineer to Order etc...) will determine how mature the lead times are. Constantly designing and sourcing new components will lead to a large volume of parts that will be bought infrequently and probably with longer lead times from the placing of a purchase order. Making the same components more often will possibly allow you to reduce purchasing lead times due to consignment stocks etc... If you are making to stock then shorter manufacturing lead times will possibly be the focus.

MRP systems largely schedule backwards from the delivery date you have accepted on your sales order. If your lead time in the system is four weeks and your order is for twelve weeks time then your system will probably not schedule any work for the next eight weeks. To get the MRP system to work properly in your business you will need a degree of trust for what it is telling you. Setting it up with the proper information is the first step to do this. Also, ensure you understand what your system is telling you. A lot of unnecessary work can be avoided if you understand how lead times are described in your system reports. This allows you to make the correct decisions based on the information provided to you.

Lead times are also not set in stone. Periodically you will want to review the lead times and make adjustments accordingly. As your business changes you will need to let your MRP system reflect the real world. Finding a fast way to do this, such as using an export / import process, as discussed in the last section, can make this a fairly painless activity.

The production lead time refers to the total amount of time required for a product to progress through the 'inside' of your business. The actual manufacturing time, plus queue times etc… make up the production lead time. So, if you issue materials to the shop floor and it takes two weeks to be despatched that is your actual production lead time. This, however, is not the value you require as the production lead time in your system for the reason outlined below.

The MRP system needs to be able to juggle the demands of various products moving through the production system at any one point in time. For this reason the system's production / manufacturing lead time needs to be longer than the actual production lead time. In reality this usually leads to a slightly longer production lead time, but allows the system to optimise the work flowing through the various work centres used to produce the work. So, this figure is the total lead time required in a fully loaded business environment plus a degree of slack.

The sales lead time is potentially a different lead time again, as this typically takes into account any backlog present in the system, plus some additional slack for processing orders, acquiring materials etc… As time progresses all of the three lead times should start to reduce, as the system becomes more effective and more accurate. Many of the problems that businesses face stem from not understanding these three different lead times and then screwing up the system trying to play catch up.

For example, if the manufacturing lead time is eight hours, the system might want three days to make the schedules work. You might give the customer a one week lead time from receipt of order and this should give you a workable system (providing stock is available). If the product in question becomes more popular and you choose to maintain finished stocks then you can adjust your lead times further (especially as the sales lead time could be zero days, if you can maintain your stocks).

For those of you who are following the Lean methodology of business improvement you may be aghast at the idea of holding stock and having bloated lead times, but this a means to an end. We will touch back on Lean toward the end of this book, but getting stability and delivery performance is our first goal, before optimising and reducing the costs present in the business.

A question that often arises when people are getting more confident with the system is 'what happens when the system's production lead time gets closer to the actual production lead time?' Whilst each system is different there is a pattern to the logic employed, and of course you would need to check this out for yourself to be fully sure of the effect. The pattern I have experienced is that the MRP system is more likely to schedule one job for completion in one go, rather than splitting the work to level out the workcentre capacity. Or, put another way, if you are getting into a backlog situation then you may want to reduce the lead times in your system so that the system tries to force work through in a 'first in first out' type approach. Again, if you are following a Lean approach and are correctly loading your business then you should be able to avoid this situation.

The purchasing lead times also need to be mentioned here. Having realistic purchasing lead times will give your Purchasing team more realistic buying schedules to work with. Exporting the purchasing data and putting it into generic buying groups will help you to update the information. Changing large chunks of data in a spreadsheet, fine tuning individual known 'problem' items, and then uploading the data can make this process far easier. Purchasing data, like all other elements of the data, need to be practical and accurate.

Lead times are critical in an MRP system and getting the right ones for your business is a priority when you want the system to work properly. Find out what you have in your system and, if they are in a complete mess, export the data and standardise the lead times into groups. Give yourself some slack, as the MRP system will work backwards to give you your start dates for production, and see if a workable plan is derived from the system. Many businesses never look back at their lead times once the system is set up and this is a mistake.

Action Steps

- Determine your lead times:

  actual production lead time;

  MRP production lead time;

  sales order lead time;

  purchasing lead times.

- Update your system information accordingly, possibly via exporting and importing the data to save time.

Horizons And Re Order Periods

The next feature of MRP systems that I want to cover is the area of batching.

Lean, as we have mentioned already, is fundamentally against batching. Whilst I agree that we only define batches because we haven't figured out a way to create our products with a near zero change over time, we need our MRP systems to reflect our current reality. As said earlier I will discuss Lean and how it can integrate with MRP systems later in this book.

For many businesses determining an economical batch size makes perfect sense. If there is demand for a component and it requires a set up time that is significant and the orders are relatively close together then making them all at the same time can be a good business decision to take. MRP systems are usually configured to accept this way of working. If we configure them correctly then we can take advantage of the benefits.

This of course does not mean that we need to take the same approach for every single item in the system, batching can be selected for individual components or for sets of components. The key here, once again, is to get our MRP system behaving the way that we want it to. Your system should reflect the logic of what a sensible person would do in the same situation. Fighting the system is counterproductive and, if you want to batch components because it makes sense, then we need to tell the system how to behave.

The two most common ways to do this are either to define minimum batch sizes in the part configuration, or to define a re-order period (or horizon). The approach you take will depend on what you forecast the ongoing demand to be and how much control you want over the upcoming production.

If you choose to use the minimum batch sizes then you will likely be producing batches that are of a similar size every time there is a new manufacturing demand placed on the system. The stock should deplete upon the despatch of new sales orders and if you have set any stock levels this will trigger new manufacturing orders. The two parameters work together in an attempt to minimise production runs.

If you choose to use the re-order periods then the system will group together existing demand in your system and create fewer larger batches. Without this set up in your system you will experience small, possibly uneconomical, production runs. If you have orders repeating within quick succession and don't want to hold stock then this can be a good way to proceed as it helps to avoid overproduction.

By reviewing the different parts that you want to consider for this kind of batching you can determine the right approach. The demo system is your friend once more; try out the different scenarios to see what works best for your parts. Try different minimum batch sizes or re-order periods and see what it does to the demand in your production order book.

The configuration of your system needs to reflect the intelligence you already have present in your business, so use this part of the system to appropriately manage the demand for specific parts and avoid using manual intervention to do the job. Manual intervention usually causes unnecessary workarounds to be created and confusion within the main system.

Set up the parts correctly!

Action Steps

- Review your repeating production items.

- Look at the demand going forward, if known.

- Test the re-order period and minimum batch quantity options in your demo system.

- Configure your repeating parts so that they are produced in a rational manner that reflects what you would do if there were no system at all.

Capacity

At the core of an MRP system is the capacity management function. It is this information that allows the system to work out when it can complete various manufacturing tasks and ultimately simulates if you will achieve the promised dates you have provided to your customers.

The scheduling function will use the information held in your capacity records, along with your routing information, to determine what can be done when. Like the other elements of this section, it is a feature that needs to be correctly set up. Let's look at the main components of the capacity element of an MRP system.

The work centres in your systems, the machines or groups of people who do the productive work, need to be reflected accurately. Many systems have different references for work centres and may split them into cells, machines and individual people operating the machines. I mentioned earlier about walking before you can run (where are you on your journey?) and less can be more when it comes to configuring your capacity settings.

I say this because there are so many factors that can affect the true capacity of a work centre. The utilisation / downtime / efficiency of a work centre can fluctuate, people may not turn up for work, you may experience a fire alarm etc... There are many external factors that can affect your working day so the aim for most is to have the capacity configuration set up so that it gives a fairly accurate picture. I suggest getting something that works and then refining it later.

Many systems have rules contained within their capacity modules. One of the common ones I have found is 'infinite capacity'. How this works precisely in your system is a matter for the demo system to explain but, in the systems I have seen it, the option allows you to override your capacity limits. If your business has an overloaded order book then this may be more of a reflection of the uneven (or inaccurate) loading of the business with production orders. We will look into accepting orders into your system later on, but what your system will do with the information once you have put it in is always good to know. Moving toward 'finite planning' is usually a goal for most businesses that operate MRP systems. This move reflects a good degree of understanding about MRP and operational control present within the business.

Your workforce will also feature in the capacity calculation, even if they are not defined in the set up as 'operator labour'. When you configure the capacity of your work centres you will need to determine a realistic capacity. Some systems will allow you to enter the utilisation factor for the process as well as the design capacity of the work centre. Throttling down the available capacity via utilisation or efficiency is something that I see being often ignored. For the majority of businesses it is unrealistic to expect that 100% of workcentre time is being used on productive work. Nevertheless, it is a goal and proper reporting can focus your improvement efforts to help you achieve it. However your system stores this capacity information you will once again be striving to mimic reality, so aim to put in meaningful information and not just figures to aspire to. You need to be realistic and use the MRP system as a tool to help you achieve higher levels of performance.

The work to list will come out of your system based on the capacity available, the quantity of parts required, the delivery date and the time allocated on the manufacturing routing. This quartet of information will ultimately provide the information your teams will use to execute the manufacturing plan. Again, I hope you can see the importance of the capacity element of the MRP system.

Many businesses use an external capacity tool to help them with their planning. The most common method I have witnessed this is via a spreadsheet. Whilst the more visual element of the spreadsheet can help people get to grips with the information contained in the system it can also cause problems if this tool falls into the 'workarounds' category that I mentioned earlier in the book. The issue I witness most often is that the capacity planning spreadsheet has the current capacity information held within it whilst the MRP system has obsolete data. This situation can lead to accurate top level schedules being scuppered by work to lists that don't reflect the requirements of the business. It is no wonder how some businesses can get their manufacturing teams so confused!

Maintenance of the capacity data is vital if you want to produce reliable and accurate work to lists, as well as being able to properly load the business in the first place. If you must have two capacity planning systems in place then make sure that they use the same information to conduct the planning with.

Action Steps:

- Configure your capacity information with up to date information.

- Include the necessary utilisation information to throttle down the capacity to mimic the realities of production.

- Determine how you can find the causes of the non-productive time and develop improvement plans to improve the utilisation.

- Add the maintenance of capacity information to your diary and keep the system up to date.

- If you have an external capacity plan review its purpose and examine the possibility of just using the MRP system to measure and plan capacity.

Scheduling Rules

The rules in the system that help it to determine what should be done when can be found in the scheduling rules. Whilst each system will have variants of the rules there are fundamentally two different approaches, forwards and backwards.

If you have experience of Gantt charts in project management then you will probably already have experienced the difference between forward scheduling and backward scheduling. Forward scheduling aims to load the work centres with work at its earliest convenience (with the intention of finishing the work as soon as possible within the manufacturing lead time that you have specified for the part).

Backwards scheduling will attempt to delay the work for as long as possible. The aim here is for a latest finish in manufacturing, ready just in time for the completion date of the works order.

For me backwards scheduling seems the most logical, holding off the production of parts until they are required. In practice there are so many companies who are in turmoil that getting the jobs started in plenty of time is a real challenge. They then end up using up the slack time and still deliver slightly later than originally planned.

If you are in a backlog situation then choosing forwards scheduling can make a lot of sense. It really is up to you and your preferences, testing the data in the demo system again is a good option to try it out for yourself. I am not indifferent however about the scheduling rules, I think it is important that we know what rules we are following and how the system is responding to our settings. It is a choice we must actively take.

Action Steps:

- Find out what scheduling rules your system is working to.

- If you are unsure of the differences then try the various options in your demo system.

- Test different scenarios, such as backlog, to evaluate what works best for your business in what situation.

BoM Accuracy

The accuracy of your Bills of Materials (BoM) should arguably be one of the first items we should have reviewed. I have however decided to leave it until now as I have been descending through the MRP configuration options moving from the broadest sections, down to the most detailed.

The BoM gives the instructions to the Purchasing team as to what they need to buy in order to provide manufacturing with enough materials to produce the products required. In some more complicated products the BoM will also stimulate manufacturing to produce components and sub-assemblies. The stores department use the BoM to pick the correct materials for a production order. The BoM also guides the production team as to how to build, or process, the main production order. Purchasing dates are usually created after the capacity plan has been created, effectively scheduling the sequence of purchases. The BoM helps to synchronise the manufacturing and purchasing activities.

Whereas other parts of the system data might be able to be exported easily, updated and then uploaded, I have always found that the BoM is a little harder to do in this way. The individual components are straightforward enough, but the structures are a different entity. Writing reports that look for specific known BoM issues is one option, but it may be that you need to review the BoMs individually.

If you are familiar with the Pareto Principle (or 80/20 rule) then you should be able to split up your products into groups based on the frequency of manufacture within your business. So, if you have a handful of products you make regularly then any inaccuracy present in their BoM will have more of an impact than a product that is rarely made.

You may choose to only review the higher volume products and specific other products in the lower volume group (i.e. known problem products). This is a management decision and you need to decide on what is right for your business.

Stock accuracy is linked to BoM accuracy, and you may already have experienced what happens when your Stock Control team issue more material than expected. If the works order is requesting less material than is required to complete the job operator experience may intervene. Manual interventions like this are common and stem back to having inadequate data in the system. The correct configuration of materials and BoMs can help businesses who are proactively looking to reduce their stockholding too.

Splitting up your products and ensuring that their BoMs are right doesn't have to be a labour intensive exercise. It can also be something that you can do over a period of time. Prioritising the quick win products (high volume / repeating products) first and then reviewing the outstanding products when they are required for new manufacturing orders can save a lot of time. Correct BoMs are vital to any MRP system working properly.

Action Steps:

- Identify your high volume (repeating) products and review their BoMs.

- Identify known problem products and review their BoMs.

- Determine an appropriate method for cleansing the other BoMs as new orders are received into your business.

Routing Accuracy

Alongside the BoM is the routing for the products. The routing is the planned sequence of steps that tells the MRP system how the product is made, and how long it takes at each stage of the manufacturing process.

A real tell tale sign of there being an issue with the routings on the system is when a works order is printed, sent to the shop floor and it refers to a machine, or piece of kit, that no longer exists! Accuracy in routings has many effects, including the morale of the people who use the output of the system!

Hopefully when you reviewed the capacity of your system you will have identified any work centres that are no longer valid and if you are unable to remove them from your system (due to linkages to accounts information) then you can at least make a list of them to identify them for removal from your routings.

To ensure that you have accurate manufacturing routings you need to make sure that each product has the right sequence of operations, on the right machines, for the correct length of time. Again this is quite often a manual process to review each routing individually but can be speeded up by writing reports that focus on key criteria (such as the obsolete work centres) or by spending a small amount of effort on the high frequency products. The same list as your BoM review can be used.

Getting the times right is essential in routings. However, some businesses just aren't sure what times should be on the routings. The extreme outcome for this is routings that display '0:00' for all of their steps. Whether you get real production time from the shop floor, use takt time to establish the correct throughput, generate generic times for the product families, or synthetic timings from work study reference guides, you need to have something put in your system that makes sense. Times can be altered in the future and process improvement / Lean activities should be striving to do this anyway. Determine the most appropriate method for choosing times and then be consistent if you don't already have times in your system.

The scheduling part of the MRP system will use the times specified in the routing information to determine how much work a work centre can get through in any particular day. I hope that your team also understands the relevancy of getting the times right in your system.

From the scheduling of the work centres comes our work to lists, these are the daily tools that your production teams can use to define what work needs to be completed on what day in order to profitably achieve the on time delivery of the production orders.

As with the BoM verification that needs to be undertaken, updating the routings is vital if they are not already accurate. Again, approaching this piece of work in a systematic way (high frequency products first) can be a relatively quick and painless process.

Action Steps:

- Review your routings for completeness and accuracy.

- If you do not have times in your system currently then consider creating generic families, or templates, to speed up this process.

- Ensure that obsolete work centres do not appear in your routings.

Stock Levels

By this point you will have possibly determined the stock levels that you want to maintain based on the decision to be a Make to Stock business or not. Stock holding decisions not only affect finished products however, they also have a bearing on the purchasing activities that take place. This part of the book may not be lengthy, but it is important; the effects of getting these settings wrong can create a lot of unnecessary work for your teams. Based on experience I will focus on the purchasing end of stock level settings.

MRP systems naturally try to make supply and demand requirements meet. This means that if we let our MRP system do what it wanted, and we hadn't set any stock levels in the system, then it would try to end with zero stock once all of the sales orders had been satisfied. What is a more common prospect is the fighting of the system's instructions and the holding of more stock than is required. If you recognise this problem in your own business let's see if we can rectify it.

No doubt your system will have a number of settings for managing stock levels against a material or bought in part. Whilst all systems are different, they have some common features.

The first of these features is the 'minimum' stock level, telling the system when it needs to purchase more material when stock falls below this level. If the lead time to purchase the material is longer than you have notice to start production then you may want to hold some stock. It is a common objective to hold no stock, but if this zero stock level prevents you from satisfying your customer's orders in an appropriate lead time then a commercial decision will need to be made in order to determine if holding stock to win business is appropriate.

The 're-order quantity' is another part of the stock settings that can help iron out other problems with your Purchasing team. If you need to purchase a particular material at 5000Kg at a time (for minimum supply etc..) and the next demand on your system is only asking for 1200Kg then it will keep telling you that it needs you to reduce your purchase order's quantity. If however you have correctly specified this in your material's setup then MRP will ignore this consideration. If you have enough of these incorrectly set up parts then your MRP suggested purchases report will be cluttered with nonsense. After enough of this nonsense there is a strong tendency for people to dismiss the reports as unusable, and you risk descending into workarounds for your purchasing activities.

As I have said elsewhere in this book, if you set up the system and the parts within the system to reflect the behaviours of the people using the system correctly, then you will receive instructions that make sense and can be worked with.

The focus of minimising stock levels is a noble one, and one that we should all strive to achieve. Jumping the gun and not reflecting on current practice is a poor approach. An optimal approach is to configure your system for the current reality, identify the simplest way to improve the performance of your business and then move on to reducing bloated stock levels.

Your physical stock levels also need to be accurate within the system. Whether your business uses cycle counting, stock takes, or low level updating (where stock levels are manually updated in your system when only a handful of product / material is available) the data in MRP needs to be current. I realise that this paragraph can have a massive impact for your business' performance, so ensure that your current method for maintaining stock accuracy works. If it doesn't, do something different.

Purchasing and stores teams are crucial to the successful supply of materials to help production complete their work. Badly set up stock levels can derail their efforts through confusion and time wasting.

Action Steps:

- Identify which materials in your MRP system require stock to be held.

- Learn what stock settings you have available to you and test them in the demo system if required.

- Make your system reflect the reality of your purchasing approach.

- Review your current method of reviewing and updating your stock levels; if it isn't effective, change it.

- Identify areas of 'stagnant' stock and develop improvement plans to use up the material and reduce overall stockholding requirements.

Summary

Teaching your MRP system how to operate is vital. From the wrong stocking levels to the wrong capacity settings, if you don't tell it how to behave it will give you something that you don't want. If you want it to become an ally and help you make good operational decisions reviewing this section and determining the right settings is a priority.

Having an accurate and reliable system helps to reduce confusion between departments through being able to supply robust information.

People waste far too much time trying to override the system, being confused by what it tells them and trying to work it out longhand. Alternatively they may spend time rectifying mistakes caused by following the bad instructions provided by the system. It was doing its best and now it is time to put the setup mistakes right.

Putting the right information into the system can make a huge leap in terms of business performance. If you are already planning certain improvements to how you work then it is possible to build these into your updating of the information. The key point I want to make is that you need your system to mimic reality so that it can be useable first.

Time will bring new information and insights with it. This new information (even if it is corrective in nature) will allow you to improve your system and the performance you gain via your system. Embrace corrections in routings and BoMs. If the current information is pushing your performance in the wrong direction then you have the opportunity to identify some process improvement projects.

Do not let your system data rot!

The next section of this book is focussed on using the MRP system properly and leans toward the management and execution of the system's instructions.

Section Three - Using It Properly

MRP systems are more than just software and hardware systems. Getting the most out of them means more than just switching on the software. There are people involved and their input is more than just pressing a couple of buttons every few minutes.

This section of the book looks at some of the supporting considerations that you will need to make as a manager. In doing so you will be able to get the most from your system; it will work for you.

A number of businesses that I have worked with have found that their expectations of their MRP system were unrealistic. They had hoped that once they had successfully set up and configured the system that would be the end of their input. Whilst this appears to be a logical assumption, there is more to it than that. There are routines and housekeeping activities that need to take place. There are mundane activities that need to be undertaken. There are times when only a human's interpretation will do. This section takes this viewpoint.

Most companies that I have worked with came to this realisation quickly. This section largely reflects the journey that they, and others, have taken. This section looks at both the core elements of the MRP output and the support activities. When combined you should find yourself at the helm of an effective system.

Work To Lists

For the production side of a business the work to list is one of the key tools. It converts the works orders and their scheduled operation dates into a usable document. Simply put, the work to list tells you what you need to do when. However, this essential element of the system is also one of the most underused in businesses that are struggling. I don't think that this is a coincidence, and this section looks to explore this point in more detail.

As work to lists are purely system driven this helps us to deal with a common issue. When the work to lists are perceived to be unreliable, or unusable, it is because of the system's configuration or loading. It can only tell you what it knows and if the system has not been set up correctly then obviously this is a problem. This knowledge gives us the opportunity to go back and correct the system, as opposed to creating a workaround.

Work to lists tell individual departments what needs to be done when. Working with the teams to ensure that they understand the format and the information is essential to make sure that they follow the instructions correctly. Sometimes a simple format change can work wonders. Other times it is just a case of working with the teams to help them grasp the concept. Although this may seem condescending, it is not intended to be so. When production teams have been used to prioritising their workloads in different ways, using a work to list may seem alien. Chasing orders based on their order value, customer status, or despatch date may have skewed their view of how a work to list is meant to work. The work to list takes into account complexity and lead times. The lists will provide sequences of work that may not seem logical to the uninitiated but you need to trust the system that you have configured. Whilst working to despatch dates (as mentioned above) seems logical it doesn't work when you have more complicated work in the middle of the schedule that needs to be started sooner. Trusting the system can be a leap of faith, but an essential one.

Using work to lists can definitely help when it comes to improving on time starts and finishes at work centres. Sharing the responsibilities of managing the work to list information between team managers / team leaders can help. When everyone is looking after their own part of the schedule via the work to lists management can become easier. One of the most difficult things to do when delivering products and services on time is to catch up when things have been started late. Starting on time (but not early) is the easiest way to achieve an on time delivery and using the work to lists to monitor this is a simple way to work. Switching the mentality from 'on time despatch' to 'on time start at work centre' can make a huge difference to how work flows through your business.

Engagement with your staff can be improved by using the work to lists. Work to lists provide an objective document to discuss progress. It is very easy to say that 'everything is OK' when asked about how production is going, even when it is not true. Even with the best organised production facilities unexpected problems occur, and even with the best planning you can still occasionally be caught off guard. Accepting this common reality means that production rarely goes perfectly, but it can be managed accordingly. If the system is configured correctly then these issues will be built into the work centre capacity information (possibly as the utilisation rating). These figures will adjust and adapt the work to lists so that the overall plan is achievable. So, whilst we don't want to deviate from the plan, we will hit bumps and we need to be open and honest about them. For as well as having problems you will most likely have other production orders that will go better than expected. The system takes in the overall mix and the 'slushy' nature of the work will balance out. With all of this in mind the work to list gives you an ideal opportunity to work closely with your team to understand the real progress being made. Developing these conversations about the real problems is a good way to develop relationships as well as improve production performance.

The feedback you receive will give you the opportunity to refine the information held in the system. In particular capacity, utilisation, labour levels and yield are good to keep updated. If you are working on your Key Performance Indicators then this information not only helps you to maintain your system but helps shape your improvement projects. Small regular improvements to your performance figures amplify through your system. Even monthly one percent utilisation improvements over a year can give you a big jump in terms of available capacity to produce orders. Use the feedback process with your work to lists to propel your bigger business based objectives.

Actual information about your production orders allows you to change course. Feedback about orders, and their lack of progress, can help you to avert late deliveries if caught early enough. If you know when milestones in production need to be achieved then feedback is more meaningful. I have seen many businesses work blind because they choose not to follow the work to lists. Their interpretation of the schedules and the subsequent poor organisation of production aren't unexpected. These businesses have not developed alternative production systems (such as Lean pull systems, which we will discuss later) to take the strain. Using the work to list as a regulatory tool to help keep everything on track is essential.

Many systems have work to lists as part of their standard offering. Many businesses modify the standard reports to suit their particular needs. This consideration becomes more interesting when you take this a step further and create bespoke versions for different departments. I'm sharing this point with you as it is one that I have experienced to be contentious in many businesses. A standard format that is used across the production teams can make a lot of sense. It is one format and therefore you don't need to decipher what you are looking at. Standardisation can bring with it a lot of benefits and suits the majority of work to list users. The request for the additional information to be supplied with the work to list is one of the main drivers I observe for creating different formats. Whilst I agree that having completely different formats is sometimes unhelpful a degree of variation can work well. If you are considering this route then consider trying an 80% standard to 20% bespoke mix. If the first part of the document (from left to right say) is standard and contains the basic information then the right hand side could contain the bespoke information. Hopefully this would work for you and give you the best of both worlds.

Work to lists can be great for a business. If you actively manage this tool then you can use the feedback to give you a real boost in terms of performance (and especially on time delivery).

Action Steps:

- Find out how well understood your work to list reports are.

- Identify opportunities for educating your team about work to list usage.

- Build work to list feedback into your regular reviews (such as a daily meeting).

- Standardise your work to lists if a bespoke format has been developed for each workcentre / department. Consider controlling the bespoke elements if they are required.

- Use the work to lists as positive feedback for improving the scheduling of production orders through the business and developing workcentre performance.

Shop Floor Data Capture (SFDC)

A core part of the MRP system that helps you to track your activities is shop floor data capture, lovingly known as SFDC. This is the part of the system that most of your production team will be familiar with. Terminals that are placed on the shop floor are used to book on and off works orders to record quantities produced and the time taken.

If you are already using this form of data entry (as opposed to an accounts clerk or similar to manually enter the data) then you will empathise with the difficulty in getting this to work in an established business. Forming the habit is key and this section offers a few ideas to help you embed this element if you are struggling to get the usage levels to where they need to be.

Having someone in the business that is dogmatic is handy with SFDC. Someone that will day in day out chase people up that aren't using the system can be a real ally. Forming habits takes time, and having someone to remind them can really help. I see many times that this kind of supervision happens for a few days and then the person reminding people stops doing it. If you choose this as your route then you need to make sure that it is unrelenting (but not oppressive) until you get the habits formed and this becomes the norm.

Another approach, building on the previous option, is to build in the SFDC usage review into a daily meeting. If you have a start of shift meeting then this could be one of your agenda items. The Team Leaders who are present at the meeting can then go and chase up the relevant team members who need to engage that day. Similar to the above item, consistency is key until you get compliance.

My third suggestion, and my favourite, is to create a demand from the shop floor to complete their bookings. If their production schedules will only update on the back of the completion of the SFDC activity then they will likely be inclined to use the system. If the Team Leaders are accountable for their production and they are being measured from MRP data then a lack of movement in the system will reflect in their scores. In one business I supported this was the only way I could make progress. The Team Leaders were supplied with Excel works order books, Sales Order books and more information than most people would need. They could muddle through OK without completing their SFDC tasks. The work to list is what they should have been working from and by taking away the other information they had to use their work to list. Guess what? The work to list was a mess until they caught up with their shop floor bookings!

SFDC feeds back the actual performance information to compare against your planned information (including costs, lead times and quality / yield). Without this information your

MRP system will not perform effectively in many areas and I urge you to review your current SFDC usage levels and accuracy. If they are not where they need to be then it may be time to improve your habits.

Action Steps

- Review your SFDC usage and accuracy levels.

- If your habits need to be improved choose an appropriate method to reinforce the need to undertake SFDC, until it becomes a sustainable habit.

- Review the data provided to make corrections in your business, from pricing to routings to utilisation ratings.

Purchase Order Instructions

As important as the work to lists are the purchasing instructions generated by the system. The big difference between the two is that the purchasing actions are less in your control. Whereas you can walk over to one of your Team Leaders and instruct them to change their schedules, it is harder with suppliers. That said, despite the disconnect and delay, your purchasing instructions can be managed in a similar way to work to lists.

The size of the task can seem enormous when you first run your purchasing reports. I have found that many people who work in purchasing teams aren't provided with enough education and training to allow them to use their tools fully. This situation can lead to under utilisation of the tools that they are given and can lead to less effective ways of working. For example I worked with one gentleman who didn't understand the purchase order range that the report was offering him. Out of fear of missing something he ran the report to cover the next eighteen months of demand. This created a very long report, but one he felt safe with. The amount of time it took him to sift through the report meant that he was only able to review the document once per week. Whilst the long range supply agreements looked good, short range operational issues were being missed. When you get into a routine and start to use the instructions generated by the system then you can find that the initial workload tends to naturally decrease.

Fighting the system is another reason why purchasing reports can be neglected. As we discussed earlier, if the information held in the system does not reflect the reality of how you purchase then your reports will be bogus. We discussed fixing these problems at the source, so I won't dwell upon it. When we combine the two issues raised in this section; overload and inaccuracy, you can see why there can be so many problems. Follow on from this with the lack of routines in many businesses and you can understand why MRP systems can be so underutilised.

Like the works orders moving through the manufacturing plant, purchase orders need to flow too. Understanding the real work content of purchase orders is essential. If your purchasing activities are not already being bundled into packets of daily work then it may be worth considering doing this. Long horizons to review purchasing requirements can lead to less frequent purchasing. Less frequent purchasing can lead to missing short range issues. Missing short range issues can lead to material being available at the wrong times. Inadequate material supply can lead to late deliveries. I'm sure you get the picture. Less intensive daily cycles that keep the material flowing in and through your business will work far better than infrequent long range planning exercises that miss the detail and result in fire fighting activities.

The information that you get back from your suppliers also needs to find its way into your MRP system. If the delivery dates of raw materials, components, sub contract parts etc. affect starting production on time, then the system must reflect this. There can quite often be a disconnect between the Production Control and the Purchasing functions of a business. Tying this ongoing communication into some form of daily meeting can help orders to be re-scheduled effectively. If the communication is early enough it is often possible to re-jig the production sequence so that you still achieve an on time delivery. This disconnect can be easier to manage if Purchasing and Production Control both report to a single Operations Manager, but is not difficult to arrange otherwise. The decision making for sourcing alternative materials, alternative suppliers or delaying production schedules can be made quickly and effectively if the information is made readily available as soon as it is known.

The purchasing instructions are critical to the running of the operation and the same amount of attention should be paid to this as to the work to list. If you don't have your materials and components ready when it is time to manufacture you can't start on time. If you don't start on time then you will find it difficult to finish on time.

Action Steps:

- Find out what purchasing reports your purchasing team are using and evaluate their usage and effectiveness.

- Review the routines and practices used in your purchasing team and consider daily cycles if not currently used.

- Link production control and purchasing together if possible to ensure smooth communication is achieved. This alone can dramatically improve your control over your operation.

Maintenance / Housekeeping

Often overlooked is the need to maintain and update the information held in your system. Simple housekeeping routines can make a tremendous difference to the usability of your system. When you have gaps in your data then you have a problem to deal with. When you have inaccurate information in your system then you need to diagnose it quickly in order to make the right decisions. Keeping the data reliable is the goal here; without this you will struggle to use the system effectively longer term.

The first step is to identify the points in data entry when errors can occur and that aren't already being picked up. The second step is to create the necessary reports that can pick up the errors. The third step is to take action and close out the gaps in the information. The fourth step is to improve the process, or provide the education to prevent the data from having gaps in it in the future. I am sure that you will be able to identify these data hot spots fairly quickly. From shop floor bookings, to purchase orders, to non-closed off sales orders, there will be a list that quickly comes to mind. You will quite possibly already have some system reports written that will help you to check your data and if you have someone in house who is good with the report writer then gaining the balance of reports should be easy.

A common sight I see, should a business have put in place maintenance / housekeeping routines, is inaction. There are two issues here. The first is when the person receiving the house keeping report (for them to correct the data) doesn't know what to do. The second issue is when the housekeeping is done in an informal way and isn't closed out properly. The first issue is easy to resolve via training and standard operating procedures. The second is also easy to resolve if you make the reports slightly more formal. If you add two signatures to the report ('issued by' and 'completed by') you will be able to tie this into a more structured approach (with possibly the Operations Manager receiving the completed reports). Inaccuracies in the data can go on for a long time and sometimes having a formal approach is the only way to get the problems resolved.

Some of the errors that you will find will be occasional mistakes, they happen. Some of the errors you find will be symptomatic of a bigger problem. Recurring errors give us the opportunity to find the underlying problems and come up with ways to improve the business. Lack of understanding, lack of skills, lack of application or whatever, can be identified and built into your improvement plans. If you start to notice trends or patterns then using the housekeeping tools will help you to correct such behaviours.

Housekeeping activities within your business need to be made routine. Some of the housekeeping routines may be daily (such as shop floor bookings, jobs on hold etc...). Some will be weekly (such as sales orders with zero balance, orphan orders etc...). Some will be monthly or quarterly (such as permissions, capacity levels, redundant work centres etc...). Identifying all of the pieces of the housekeeping jigsaw and the short corrective actions required is all it takes to create your own housekeeping routine. Building it into other routines you have can make it easier to adopt for your business.

Identifying learning opportunities from the housekeeping is invaluable. If your team don't understand why they are doing certain things in a certain way then you have the opportunity to explain it to them. There is a big difference between having enough knowledge and not enough. Make housekeeping a part of the regular management of your system and you will benefit not only from a better set of data in your system but more competent users also.

Action Steps:

- Identify the areas where the data in your MRP system is poor.

- Create the necessary reports to pull out the corrections you need to make.

- Consider a formal system to close out the errors and provide training to the people causing the errors as appropriate.

- Develop the housekeeping routines and build them into your working life.

SOPs

Standard Operating Procedures (SOPs) exist in most businesses in one form or another. Their ability to be used by an organisation successfully however is an altogether different matter. The learning we get from our MRP systems as we update and change the system needs to be crystallised somehow into our business and SOPs are a simple way to catch the learning, speed up training and regulate future improvement activities.

Many businesses write their new SOPs when they are learning how the system works on a demo version. The training phase and the execution phase are clearly different. Re-writing the SOPs after the training phase is essential as there is so much additional learning that takes place once a system goes live. That said, writing SOPs during the training is far better than not writing them at all. Unfortunately however, many businesses expect to work properly, and consistently, based on rambling notes held on spiral bound jotter. SOPs needn't be overly complicated; step by step instructions is all they are, but ones that are clear and objective. The test is if someone who doesn't have any prior knowledge of the system can follow them and execute the instructions then it's a good instruction. If you don't have SOPs then doing some research and developing a format that works for you is a good plan.

If you haven't yet been convinced by the idea of SOPs, then consider your new starters, and the holiday cover you require. Time and time again I have witnessed that businesses that have decided to take their SOPs seriously find that training time is slashed. The new person who joins the team does not have to learn second hand bad habits. The person who is loaned for an afternoon can become productive in a very short period of time. Including your MRP activities into your SOPs can give you the same benefits. SOPs should not be seen as part of a Quality Management System only.

One of the reasons that businesses purchase MRP systems is to get control over processes and speed up how things are done. SOPs support this approach by letting you have better control by using the same methods to get the same results when performing a process or task. Any changes that you make to your usage of your MRP system need to be documented. Revision control on the SOPs can help you to manage the changes in a process as well as helping you to manage the introduction of change. Grouping changes together and not allowing changes to just appear in your business is important. Changing the approach to how you operate your MRP system is also important. One small change of a setting in MRP can dramatically affect the output and alter the instructions that are required. Control in this context is essential.

As I said earlier, testing new parts of a system leads to learning. Learning provides stepping stones to higher levels of performance. Reflecting periodically against the SOP as a means to identify opportunities for improvement is important. It is very easy to ignore SOPs once they have come into existence; it is another thing to use them to springboard the performance of your MRP system periodically. Dust off your SOPs and check to see if you have coverage for your MRP activities. If you don't then it is time to find out just how useful they can be.

Action Steps:

- Find out where your business is in terms of using SOPs.

- Review your SOPs for MRP tasks, identify the gaps.

- Write the outstanding SOPs and test them with people who are not familiar with the processes.

Routines

I have touched on routines earlier in this book. When you operate a system, the routines you deploy are critical. Every part of the system needs to be operated and updated in specific ways. This section of the book looks in a little more detail at the necessity of routines.

When you pull apart a system to examine the components and related tasks you will see key points in a process. Specifying how and when you want to trigger these key points will ultimately define your routine. Building routine and discipline into your business on the back of a series of daily, weekly, monthly and quarterly activities can make a huge difference to performance. In fact, this one element alone has accounted for many of the turnarounds I have seen in on time delivery performance.

Getting in to a habit is essential, once a routine has been defined. The ability to define a routine and to execute it are two different things. Forming good habits, as I am sure you are aware, is not the easiest thing to do. Supporting those who need to make the changes is essential and sometimes it can be a case of cajoling people. Making sure that your team understand the importance of developing the habit is the key. If they don't understand why it needs to become a habit then you will struggle to make the change. If the link can be made between what the habit is and why it helps the business then your chances will improve. For every change in terms of routine you need to make sure that you can explain the knock on effect of both doing it and not doing it.

Resistance to forming a new habit can often oscillate around performing a task each and every day. If the task doesn't take long to complete then a common argument is that doing a bigger batch once a week is easier. You will need to evaluate this on the particular tasks' merits. My view on this is that is better to complete a task at the point of origin, and perform small tasks each day than one big task at the end of the week. If the information in the system is being updated more often then the system is healthier. If you miss one day then you can catch up more easily and if it only takes a small period of time then where is the problem? With all of the hustle and bustle of working life, days can be written off. If a written off day contains your 'batched' actions then it becomes harder to catch up. It is up to you to help maintain the standard of data in your system and small daily tasks usually outweigh larger batched activities when it comes to routine MRP system tasks.

Leading on from daily tasks is the idea of daily 'course' corrections. If every day we are making small corrections to keep our production on track, then it is a manageable task. When we leave the changes for a period of weeks then we find that correcting the data is big task. The task can then appear to be so big that we put off doing the said task and the situation can get worse and worse. You can tell that I am a big fan of daily routines and hopefully you can see why. Getting the essence of what you are meant to do with your MRP system and then creating the necessary daily routine (and supporting routines of longer periods) can make a big difference. The purchasing actions, the shop floor data, the scheduling and the issuing of materials are just a few of the areas that can benefit. Starve any one of these functions from their daily updates and it can cause a knock on effect in the business:

- Late start of jobs from late issuing of materials.

- Late issuing of materials from late ordering from suppliers.

- Confused schedules from poorly updated work centres.

You get the idea.

If you are struggling to think of what your routines need to be then it can useful to map out your process. Map it out from the perspective of MRP. Move from enquiry to quotation to sales order input etc… At each step in the process there will be a critical action. What is it? List these out and you will likely have the basis for your routine. Taking these critical actions and phrasing them as an intelligent statement is your next step. 'Buy materials' may become 'daily clearance of all new recommended purchase orders'. 'Sales Order Processing' may become 'enter all new sales orders onto the system in line with the contract review dates'. By doing this you should hopefully build a more complete picture of what your routines need to look like.

One of the simpler, and effective, ways to develop the necessary habits is to piggy back other routine actions. For example, if you have a daily meeting (such as a start of shift brief) then adding in the checks for the new routines becomes simple. If every day you ask your team if their tasks from yesterday have been completed it can help to enforce the right behaviours. New habits do take time to form and if you can find an existing mechanism to help you then all the better. There are other ways too. Visual management systems (including Kamishibai boards) work well as reminders. Electronic calendars can work for many people too; it is all about finding some kind of daily prompt that can help forge new habits.

As time moves on it becomes important to periodically review and reflect upon the routines that have been established. Elements of the business will change and this will likely have a knock on effect on the routines. What was effective last year will possibly no longer serve you. Find these changes and update the routines accordingly. Of course this will need to be done in a controlled manner as changing routines needs to be done systematically. I have experienced a number of companies that would rather re-invent the wheel than form the necessary habits. Locking down routines (like the SOPs discussed earlier) can save you from heartache and miscellaneous changes being put in place. Stability, discipline and routine cannot be underestimated in the process of making your MRP system really work.

Action Steps:

- Map out your process from an MRP perspective.

- Identify the key points in the process and determine how often these elements need to be completed.

- Create a daily agenda of 'process checks' and build into a regular (existing) daily meeting.

- Work with your team to develop the necessary habits.

Discipline / Visual Management And Abdication

As you are probably aware, or have at least gathered from this book, running a system requires discipline. Time and time again I see businesses that make the necessary system changes then let go of the reins again. When you decide how you want your MRP system to operate then you need to also consider how you want to keep control. There are many methods of doing this, and you need to find the ones that suit you.

On top of the routines we have talked about we have our policies. These are the principles that keep our system in order. Whereas our Standard Operating Procedures may talk about how to input a sales order, our policy may dictate what level of capacity we can operate at. These rules of the system need to be adhered to in order for the system to work properly and help us to have (slightly) easier lives whilst profitably delivering our products on time. Auditing is a simple way to do this, choosing specific elements of the business and finding out how they are operated. If your team are following the instructions and keeping within the rules of the system then you can move to the next area. If they are not then you can choose to work with the team in a remedial way. Auditing helps to keep your finger on the pulse and finds areas of improvement. Rules can be changed and this method can help to highlight what needs to be changed. Rules can bring with them rigidity, but also control. Use rules (or policies) wisely to steer the performance of your system.

Many systems today have graphical dashboards with them. These visual representations of the performance of your system can be invaluable to management. I have noticed that many businesses have reports and Key Performance Indicator information available, but that it goes unused. Reports that tell you what you need to do in order to improve performance lie untouched. Dashboards on the other hand summarise data brilliantly. You can use the dashboard to drive your focus to the right report at the right time. So instead of having to check several reports a dashboard can help point you in the right direction and save you time. Even if you don't have a glitzy automated dashboard you can often create one using a report writer. A one page summary of key metrics can do wonders and is certainly worth investigating. For those of you who don't think you have access to these tools there is another solution. Find someone who works for you and get them to compile the information each day and give it to you. This is not my favourite option, but if it gets the job done then it could be worthwhile investing the time. Remember, a good route to take is effectiveness first and then efficiency.

Whilst all of this day to day work is going on I feel that it is important that the manager of the team has a good grasp of the team's work. An appreciation of how your team conduct their work means that better decisions can be made when processes need to be changed. I am not suggesting that you need to learn the jobs inside out, but a basic understanding of what the jobs are can really help. In MRP systems there are a lot of interconnected elements. Adjusting one part of the system can affect other areas and having a view of this can help improve the quality of decisions. Hopefully this book has been able to shed some light on the inner workings of MRP too.

As a manager you need to make sure that the people are keeping within the parameters defined that help the system to work. Largely the main driver for keeping the system working is the accuracy of the information held in the system and the correct loading of the capacity. Too many times I have seen managers abdicate responsibility for this. Systems need monitoring; elements (such as the housekeeping activities) need to be corrected periodically. Making these checks shouldn't take up too much time, but you do need to find a way to build the checks into your working life.

Action Steps:

- Identify how you can keep 'your finger on the pulse' with your MRP data.

- Gain a basic appreciation of the MRP tools as a minimum.

- Track the performance of your production and your MRP data, using a dashboard or similar.

- Delegate responsibility, but don't abdicate. MRP systems help achieve performance, but they don't do it on their own.

The Manual Reschedule – Taking The Pain (And Learning)

If at this point in the book you have realised that you are simply stuck then it may be time to go back to basics. No matter how much you re-configure your system, if your order books are overloaded then you need to straighten them out. This of course assumes that your system is not capable of doing it automatically. If your system needs to be manually rescheduled then it is a case of taking the pain and learning from it.

For the majority of systems the first port of call is to look at your sales order book. The sales order delivery dates drive the works order completion dates and the purchase order dates. Getting the sales orders into the right order, consuming the right amount of capacity is the name of the game. The capacity reports / tools that you have in your system will help you to view the effect of your re-scheduling. Knowing your real capacity, and having the right information in your system set up, is therefore essential before you start this task. Also, I recommend that you don't just move orders without understanding what you are moving. Some orders will be work in progress and possibly worth leaving where they are. Other orders may have special requirements that may be best off left too (such as expensive materials that have already been ordered). Consultation with your customers is also a good move as they may shed some light on their true priorities when it comes to deliveries. The point is clear. Use your intelligence and communicate prior to ripping apart the order book and rescheduling the sales orders.

This kind of long hand planning shouldn't need to be undertaken again, unless some major incident stops you in your tracks (such as a fire in the factory), so take it as an opportunity to learn.

- How did you end up in this position?

- How would you prevent this happening again?

- What do we need to change in the system?

Unfortunately, I have seen numerous businesses that have made the manual reschedule a monthly event, zapping morale and never getting them out of the loop. Please take advantage of the opportunity to learn from your past mistakes.

The learning and insights gained should allow you to re-configure your system, to prevent a reoccurrence. From the previous sections of this book you should be able to find the relevant elements of your MRP system and then plug in the various changes. One area of change that many people need to look at after doing this exercise is the way that their staff handle incoming orders. This is looked at in more detail in the next section. When a business fails to load their orders correctly (using erroneous information regarding capacity or otherwise) it usually creeps up and bites them after a while. The other elements such as work centre capacities should be updated as part of this exercise and then built into housekeeping routines accordingly.

Once the changes have been made it is advisable to set a date in the diary to see how things are looking. A week's gap initially is a good period of time to perform the evaluation. This length of time is not too long to manage if there is still a deviation between the actual performance and the planned performance. Once you are happy with what is going on then you can relax this review whilst you ensure the changes are correct. Of course, if the changes aren't correct you have the opportunity to revise the configuration and go through the review cycle again.

The manual re-schedule is a pain, but sometimes it has got to be done.

Action Steps:

- If your order book still has a backlog / overloaded periods after re-configuration of the system then a manual re-scheduling exercise is required.

- Use your capacity tools to help you schedule out the orders.

- Use your knowledge and intelligence to move the right orders.

Don't move orders indiscriminately if it can be avoided.

- Find the learning points from the re-scheduling exercise. What can be improved upon? What can be changed?

Contract Review / Order Input Decision

As mentioned in the previous section, the contract review element of accepting orders can make a huge difference to those businesses that experience huge sways in order types. From variations in volume, product mix and staff, a solid contract review can help many businesses move from poor levels of on time delivery performance to the best in class very quickly.

The fundamental issue when undertaking, or designing, a contract review is the ability to load 'buckets' of capacity in the future. This means that in preparation for introducing such a process you need to have capacity information available for the meeting that is accurate and up to date. There is also a lot of confusion about MRP type scheduling and Lean production systems. Even with a Lean production system you need to be able to regulate what comes into the system. We discuss linking the two systems later on in the next section of this book

To determine whether an order can be accepted (or rejected, or negotiated) you need to create a simple agenda. The agenda can be based on the decision flow you would naturally go through to accept an order. My view on why this isn't done is down to perceived time. When people are put under pressure corners can often be cut. If there is no implication to the cut corner then it can become the norm, and you end up with a different process. Your agenda should help to navigate this problem by introducing a level of formality (and speed) into the acceptance process.

The flow chart could include:

- Engineering: New product introduction / support requirements
- Purchasing: Material availability / treatments / lead times
- Capacity: Routing choice / resource required
- Quality: Past issues / special inspections

Converting your flow chart into a 'Yes / No' series of questions can help to turn your flow chart into a meaningful (and short) meeting agenda. An example agenda, based on the points above, may look like:

- Is this a new product?
- Do we need additional Engineering support?

(If 'yes', how much time do they need?)

- Are the materials available?

(If 'no', what is the lead time for the materials?)

- Based on the current availability of materials and input from Engineering, do we have capacity to manufacture?

(If 'no', when is the first availability?)

- Are there any treatments required?

(If 'yes', what is the lead time?)

- Are any special inspections required?

- Is this revised date in line with the customer's requirements? (If 'no', speak to the customer to negotiate dates)

To make the contract review process work you need to get the right people together, at the right time, with the right information to ask the right questions. The formality in the process doesn't suit every business, but it is about creating a robust process. I've seen businesses that only pay lip service to this part of the order intake and I've seen the chaotic results when they have a degree of complexity in their order books. This is just one part of the balancing of resources and orders equation (or, supply and demand).

Many MRP systems have 'What If' planning functionality in them. This allows the system to simulate what would happen if you put these orders into the system. Providing you have the system set up correctly then this tool can help to speed up the process of contract review. That said, it is quite often the handful of oddball orders that really screw up the capacity in work centres. If you can see this kind of situation occurring in your business then you could consider streaming the incoming orders. Some could be entered onto the systems if they are low risk (i.e. what is commonly known as runners or repeaters) using only a checklist. Other more difficult items (i.e. the strangers) may need to go through the more formal process as a meeting with the relevant attendees.

I accept that most businesses have some form of contract review process. My question to you, based on the companies I have assisted, is 'how accurate is your process?'

Action Steps:

- Find your contract review process, if it exists, and question its effectiveness.

- If the process needs to be overhauled then map out your decision making process to accept a new order and build an agenda around that.

- For differing levels of product complexity consider streaming the contract review process. Less complex products could use a checklist at sales order inputting time. More complex products may need to go through a more formal meeting to accept the order.

Summary

From reading this section of the book I hope that you have now considered some non-system issues. The main point I want you to take from this section is that configuring a system and then leaving it alone isn't enough.

Once the system is working correctly you need to build routines that help your team interact with the system and the information effectively. Writing SOPs (Standard Operating Procedures) can help speed up the training of new staff and allow you to keep a degree of control over the repeatability of the processes being used.

The execution of the work to lists and the purchase order requirements naturally fit into the routines. SFDC is paramount to a system that works and the right habits need to be developed. Housekeeping routines to maintain the quality of your data form part of these effective routines too.

From a management perspective you need to consider how you want to manage the MRP process going forwards. Dashboards can work well and are well worth looking into, to give you a snapshot of the process.

And, when the re-configuration still leaves you with a bump in your order book, there's the need to manually re-schedule. Although painful at first, when combined with a good contract review process and ongoing management, having to repeat this can be avoided later on.

Each part of the system offers you feedback, plus the opportunity to improve how your business operates. Please take the supporting elements from this section of the book and use them to help you further improve how your system works.

In the next section of this book I will look at a number of points related to running an MRP system. These points should help you to extend your own plans as to how to improve the performance of your business via MRP.

Section Four – Making Further Progress

So far in this book we have covered how to approach your MRP system's usage, its configuration and how to use it effectively. This section of the book looks at a number of related issues that can help you going forward.

The topics I will cover include looking for opportunities to automate information, using exception reporting, and developing your team. As mentioned previously I will also look at linking MRP with Lean, how to manage your ongoing performance and improving your relationships with other departments.

Automation

MRP systems naturally lend themselves toward automation. They're designed to take out the donkey work from trying to juggle thousands of demands and they do it well. As discussed at the start of this book, workarounds and bad practices can creep into daily working life. There is the opportunity to look at what your team is doing and figuring out if there is a better way to perform the task.

To get started it is advisable to perform a Pareto, or 80/20, review of the administration tasks that are being performed. The 80/20 rule states that a minority of tasks will take up the majority of the time used. So, if you can identify the couple of time consuming tasks to improve you will get a better return on your invested efforts. Compile a list of the tasks performed and the total time used to complete each task over a period of time (month, or quarter for example). Rank the list in terms of the time used (from largest to smallest) and you will have your prioritised list.

For each item in your list you will need to find out how the task is performed currently. For each step in the process you have the opportunity to question how it is done and try to find a better solution. This process is the basis of most process improvement activities, but in this context you are able to consider your MRP system as part of the solution. Sometimes you will find out that people are performing tasks 'by hand' when there is an unused module in the system. Sometimes the tasks are irrelevant to current working practices and sometimes you will need to find a half-way house to improve the situation. For those times that you are unable to find an answer directly from your system you may need to be slightly more creative. Although spreadsheets are often a workaround option for many businesses they can be a good solution when used properly. If there is no system solution for your issue then exporting can be used to good effect, often into a spreadsheet. This kind of approach is especially common when trying to create some form of management information and the output, or manipulation of data, is not possible via the system. The smartest options I generally see are when data is imported via a data link into a pre-defined spreadsheet. The data is then categorised and sorted by the pre-defined elements and the amount of time required to manipulate the data is minimised. If you have spreadsheet gurus in your business then a clearly defined specification is the other half of the equation.

Report writing is a lesser step than having data links designed and is often simpler and faster too. The point is that if you look into the tasks you and your team are undertaking there is often opportunity to save time and effort. Using your brain to generate alternative methods of working is the point. My list of options, in preference, is listed below:

- Delete task / stop performing them.

- Find system alternative.

- Export data / data link to perform task faster.

- Delegate task.

- Think harder!

I have put 'think harder' because 'stay as I am' looks too defeatist!

Every process can be improved if you have enough knowledge and time to apply yourself. I hope that this part of the book stirs you to go and find what else your MRP system can do to help you and your team.

Action Steps:

- Identify where the bulk of time is spent in your MRP system.

- Use the above review sequence to streamline your tasks.

- Work on the highest volume / most time consuming task first and work down your list.

Managing By Exception

When you are managing a growing set of data in your MRP system it can become a time consuming task. If the task gets too big then it is quite possible that it becomes a task that gets avoided. This is bad news if it is part of a critical process! This situation gets even worse when it is not recognised that the process is critical until something goes wrong.

Have you been in a meeting where someone has trawled through a large set of data / printout to try and see what is happening? I have and I'm sure that most people reading this book have too. I have been that person trawling through the data in the past, have you been that person too?

Exception reporting is a logical progression from trying to manage everything to just managing the things that need to be managed. By defining a handful of critical points in our processes we can then find ways to get the little bit of information that is needed in order to manage the process. I used to watch Production Managers scouring every single line on their order book to help manage their operations. I decided in one job that this took too long and got a report written that told me which operations had not been triggered on time. Within moments I could walk over to the right area of production and have the right discussion with the right person. Again, this is an opportunity to increase our personal effectiveness via the system.

I'm not saying that you need to forget everything else in your business, but tying ourselves up in knots to get a minimal level of performance is not a great idea either. There are so many other projects and tasks that add more value that we could be doing instead of low level activities like manually sifting data.

An ex-colleague of mine used to spend all week maintaining a list of production parts. The list was always out of date due to the nature of production moving whilst the list was being compiled. He kept on maintaining the list because that was what he always did. When that person left and I inherited that job (on top of my existing responsibilities of course) and I automated it. The system could track this information and by defining the specific points in the process that I needed to take action on a simple system based report would do the hard work for me.

What are the critical points in your processes and how can you manage by exception?

Action Steps:

- Map out the key points in your production process and make them areas of focus.

- Find, or create, tools that will help you to manage these critical points far more efficiently and effectively than they currently are.

- Don't lose track of the other data in the business, but do use your new found time to progress other projects that are more valuable to the business longer term.

System Privileges

MRP 'system privileges' is a funny topic in my mind due to the bi-polar approach I see in industry. On one hand there are companies who tie everything down from day one and people never find out what is available. On the other hand there are companies who leave it open and an 'I can do this myself' approach can ensue, leading to data problems and lack of clarity regarding ownership.

For those who have slacker settings on their systems I have noticed that their live system and their demo system have the same settings. I like the approach of using the demo system to get acquainted with a system, to fully appreciate the breadth of options, before locking down the privileges. This is a happy medium, giving you control and the ability to properly define the privileges for your system.

Staying with those companies who prefer the slacker approach to their settings consider the consequences. If you have helpful people in your business who can lend a hand that is great. The problem arises when these same people are effectively interfering with production via MRP whilst thinking that they are helping. Re-dating sales orders, shuffling production orders, placing purchase orders etc... Keeping control of these functions is essential. When people move from one role to another it is definitely worthwhile amending their privileges. There is a difference between flexibility and uncontrolled 'help'.

If you haven't checked your system privileges and need to tighten them up then creating template roles for your business can make a lot of sense. Each job role in your business will require a specific set of access rights / privileges. As new people join the business the settings can be replicated. Resetting people's privileges may ruffle a few feathers at first, but overall it will be worthwhile putting the control back in place.

Action Steps:

- Conduct an audit of your system user's privileges.

- Create template privilege settings for specific job roles if appropriate.

- Correct your user's privileges to provide the right level of access for each user's area of responsibility.

Develop The System Not The Workarounds

Right through this book I have talked about developing the system and not just accepting the way things are. Managing this process is essential in order to keep momentum and get results. This section will look at some ideas that you can use if you don't have a method already.

Finding the problem areas is usually not too hard. Complacency can be a real problem when investigating areas for improvement. Many people will minimise the problems in their work area when they feel that they are being scrutinised. When they take it personally they often put up their defences blocking the issues from view. You may already know what needs to be worked on and if so that is great. If you don't then you will need to work with your teams to understand which parts of the process can be improved.

Finding solutions to the problems is the next challenge. Hopefully some of the answers will be contained in this book. Others may be found by playing with the demo system, working with other departments or asking the software vendor's help desk. Properly defining the problem makes identifying a solution far easier and it is worth taking the time to do this if answers aren't forthcoming.

As part of the investigation to find out what the problem is you will be subjected to new information and insights. This learning can often be beneficial to the business and should be built into the business where possible. The objective of improving the system is that the business gets better and better over time. Standard Operating Procedures, which we discussed earlier, are a good way of capturing these items.

Large change projects can scare a lot of people. For this reason I like to use 'mini projects' with my clients. Even though there may be ten mini projects (as opposed to one large project) this more palatable approach can help to get the projects off the ground. If you are not familiar with this approach then looking up 'Kaizen' on the Internet may help. Small steps help to get projects moving and then natural momentum can help to take the project through to completion; it's all about confidence with the people delivering the project work. Like all good projects, it is good practice to include who is doing what, when they will do it by and how much time it will take to complete the task. Managing the project then becomes the main task, keeping your finger on the pulse as the elements of the mini projects get completed.

Before you design your mini project there will possibly have been some Key Performance Indicators (KPIs) that you had noticed. If your project aims to directly influence these KPIs (i.e. improve the performance in specific ways) then keep an eye on them. If you have project meetings then use these KPIs to open up the meeting and discuss which way they are moving. Over the course of the project, and beyond, you should be able to correlate what you did with the change in the KPIs. Use them as your compass to assess the impact of what you are doing / have done.

Make the system work for you. Play the long game of business process improvement rather than finding quick fixes and workarounds. It will be worth it in the long run.

Action Steps:

- Identify the problem areas.

- Correctly state the problem (which identifies the appropriate course of action).

- Develop (mini) projects to tackle the problem.

- Find the relevant KPIs and use them as an objective guide to the impact of your improvement activities.

- Execute your plans.

Auditing

I have already touched upon the importance of avoiding abdication from management responsibilities once the changes have been made. Auditing is a simple and effective way to keep the good practises in place once established.

There are two points I want to raise regarding conducting an internal audit of your MRP system and supporting activities. Firstly, you need to check and see if the technical aspect of the job is being done correctly. Secondly, you need to check and see if the style is right (on time, with right people etc...). Fundamentally, are your team doing what they are meant to be doing?

You may want to wait for a short time after making the changes to your system before you commence auditing. After the processes and routines have settled down that it is the time to see what is going on. After a period of formal change it becomes normal to relax. Your team will likely have become comfortable with the revised way of working and it is this point when bad habits can creep in. Six months is the longest I would leave it before checking back up on a process, and two months is more realistic.

If you have followed the action points in this book you will be well aware of the key points within your system that you want to audit. Determine the key points if you haven't already, this will be the focus for your audit. I recommend that you have an audit form to use; it makes comparing progress from the last audit easier. You also have to choose how you want to evaluate each point. I work with my clients to define a scale, with the early points (on a 10 point scale) being made up from the technical perspective. The remaining points are made up according to the style of delivery. For example, is it done with enthusiasm and engagement with the team?

If you are measuring KPIs as part of your audit (to provide an objective edge) then the whole scale will be made up from the objective measure. Your scale however does not need to be linear. If you are measuring on time delivery performance the first couple of points on the scale may only take you to 70% on time. The later points could refer to increasingly hard to reach targets. In this example 98%+ may be the top score, instead of 100%. The purpose of your scale is to offer a degree of overall objectivity for the processes being reviewed and consistency for comparison.

Building the audit process into your routines is vital if you want this approach to be meaningful. Completing the audit once can give you a good view of what happens. Doing it twice can help you plot the trajectory of the improvement. Doing it consistently gives you a mechanism to review performance. Once you have corrected some poor ways of working you may choose to relax the auditing frequency. I suggest that you start on a monthly cycle and then consider moving to quarterly once you have developed the appropriate habits that serve the business.

If the audit is taking too long, or if it is becoming stale, then change the format. A simple way to do this is to define what are the core items to be reviewed (that you will review at each audit) and what are optional items (that you will rotate). Having a slightly different format will keep it more engaging for your staff and reduce preparation that could be done beforehand (when the audit timing is known in advance). The purpose of doing it this way is not to catch your staff out, but to gain a wider and more diverse view of how the business processes are working.

Each time you audit your business in this manner you have the opportunity to find areas to improve. Rather than using the audit as a conduit for beating up your staff, use it to find out what can be improved. Combine the issues raised with some root cause problem solving, such as the '5 Why' approach, and you will quickly find that you have some improvement plans that are worth following. Sometimes you will find that the cure to the issue is educational. People forget how to do things, use your internal mentors / leaders and your SOPs to correct this situation.

When you have completed your audit, and I will assume that

your scale moves from left (poor) to right (excellent), you can make it visual for your team. If you get a coloured pen and draw a line through the scores you will get a visual indicator. The aim of the game is to get your line to move from left to right. Often a simple little addition, like a red line on an audit, helps to get better buy in from the team to the work that needs to be done.

Auditing is a simple yet powerful tool to help you keep the right type of activity in place.

Action Steps:

- Create a list of audit points in your MRP process. These may be the same as your routines / daily meeting agenda points.

- Devise a scoring system (1 to 10 is a good scale) and consider making it non-linear so that the later points are progressively harder to achieve.

- Rotate elements of the audit if it becomes stale, but maintain a core group of items that get reviewed each time.

- Explain the results to your team and develop improvement projects on the back of this.

- Compare results from one audit to another to gauge a direction of travel.

Backup

At this late stage in the book I would hope that your backup method is in place for your system's data. However, in the spirit of not assuming anything, we will quickly run over some points regarding backups.

There are three main points that I want to cover:

1 – Is the data worth backing up?

2 – Can you retrieve your data should you need to?

3 – Are your backups working properly?

The data being stored needs to be worth backing up. If you have established proper ways of working and you have introduced your housekeeping routines then you should be able to answer this question. If you haven't then this may be a good time to run the data through some filters / users and see what state it is in.

Next, should something go wrong with your system, can you get the data restored easily. Many businesses have tested this thoroughly and others haven't. Knowing what to do when the system falls over, or gets corrupted, is a good drill to practice.

Finally, do you check your backups from time to time? I once met a business where all four different backup methods had failed. One by one they had fallen over; it was only when something went really wrong that they found out the magnitude of their problem. Like any other system, maintenance, routine and housekeeping are essential.

MRP data is as vital as any other data in your business. If it is not part of your IT backup strategy then please make sure it gets in there soon.

Action Steps:

- Ensure your MRP data is being backed up regularly.

- Integrate with your existing IT backups as appropriate.

- Test your backups periodically to ensure that your data is retrievable.

Ongoing Education

When your system was introduced was the background to MRP, the way it works, explained? Quite often training for a new system being implemented is focussed on how to complete the basic input functions rather than how the system works as a whole. Whilst knowing how to complete the rote steps of the system tasks is essential, as time goes on it can help for people to understand how MRP works generally.

It can be argued that the system operators do not need to know how the whole system works. However, in a controlled environment this additional knowledge can provide some much needed context to make better decisions. Having a better understanding of why changes need to happen makes them easier to implement. And, as long as the privileges are correct, this should not have an adverse effect on the system. As mentioned in the section on privileges, a little bit of knowledge and the flexibility to fiddle can be a real problem. The kind of education I am referring to is to help people do their job better because they understand why they are doing what they do.

Although MRP has been around in since the mid 1970s, the new people that are joining your business might not necessarily appreciate or understand how the system works. There might also be established members of your team who are in the same boat too. Creating a series of short talks / presentations about how the system works can be a good idea. Being able to explain how one person's output becomes another person's input and what the system does in between can be really useful. When the penny drops as to why people are doing what they are doing it can make adherence to the system's rules easier.

From having better knowledge of how the system is designed to work, better feedback can be given back by the users. This can be used to fine tune parts of the system, or to identify mini projects to aid further development. Education can be used to draw out good ideas and develop the business' performance. I often meet businesses that have staff that know their bit inside out, and do it well, but don't appreciate their part in the overall picture. In the next section I am going to share with you a method to help improve this position. For now though I want to leave with you the idea that once you have your system working right it can be backed up with some educational work that can help you leap to a new level of performance. This book is generic. Your team and system are yours. It will ultimately be the ideas generating from within your business that will make the biggest gain.

Action Steps:

- Create a series of mini talks about how the inputs and outputs of various parts of your MRP system work.

- Invite questions about how the system works to identify areas for internal training.

- Ask your team to deliver short overviews of what they do in their job, explaining how they use system information to complete their tasks.

Developing Your Approach For The Other Teams

One of the trickiest issues when working in a larger business with MRP is getting support from other departments. This could be the subject of many books in their own rights, but I want to offer you a simple approach that can help to improve performance. If you can get other departments to understand how they interact with your department (and vice versa) changes become obvious and easier to implement. You will then know how the other teams work and what their challenges are. This option is to help facilitate the right conversations to make the system work better overall. If you oversee a number of teams then this approach can also be used, but facilitated by the managers of each team rather than by yourself.

The method I offer can be replicated by each department in turn.

Step 1 – Gather your team.

Bring your team together to explain the purpose of this 'workshop'; to find out where the main interactions are with the other departments and what improvements we can identify. Ideally the whole of your team should be present for the workshop.

Step 2 – Draw a spider diagram.

On a large piece of paper (or whiteboard) draw a circle representing your team in the middle. Around the edge of the paper list the other departments that you work with. Spread them out evenly around the paper if possible.

Step 3 – List interactions / capture issues.

Starting with a department of your choice start to list all of the interactions that your department has with them. If you supply them with information then put those interactions in one list. If they supply you with information then list that too. For each of these interactions it is worth capturing any issues you have with each item on your list. Don't analyse the issues, just list them. Add in any additional notes or comments as you see fit.

Step 4 – Repeat step 3 for remaining departments.

This will give you a comprehensive view of your interactions with the other departments.

*** Special Care Point ***

When you have a list of issues that you want to raise with other departments be careful. I have seen this go wrong when taken at face value. If you are looking to get some cooperation to improve then be gentle. Firstly, no one likes being told they are doing a bad job and confronting them about this list is quite unpalatable to most. Secondly, the list may want to be reviewed. In my experience there are three types of item on the lists that get created.

The first group are completely off the mark. They are based on hearsay and perception and don't adequately reflect the reality of the situation. The second group are items that aren't clear cut. There may be some truth to the items, but they need to be refined from their current state in order to be worked on. The final group are spot on. These items are good to go and can be discussed as they are.

We will sort the three groups out in a moment, but I wanted to draw your attention to this issue. If you, or your team, start blazing arguments about issues that aren't accurate then future collaborative improvement work is a lot more difficult. I have seen those who have approached this bluntly and those that have approached the same situation tactfully. Considered tactful approaches unsurprisingly yield better results.

Step 5 - Review concerns.

For each of the items on your list you will need to evaluate the underlying issues. If you are familiar with the 5 Why approach then that can be a really good tool to use. Otherwise dig around the subject, get the supporting information, and find out what is causing the issue. As with 5 Why, don't accept the first answer as being the solution. Keep digging past the symptoms until you find something solid and concrete that you can work with. You will know when you have reached a workable point as the solution will seem blindingly obvious once revealed.

Performing this activity will help you to segregate the different groups of issues. When you get the supporting information then you will be able to eliminate the incorrect issues and firm up the real issues in the second group.

Step 6 – Meet with department heads.

Now that you have a list of issues to discuss with each department it is time to arrange the meeting. If you have undertaken this exercise as an entire business then the simplest way to arrange these meetings is in advance, to a timetable. When everyone knows that these meetings are going to take place then it becomes far easier to hold the meeting. If you are performing this exercise on your own you have singled yourself out and you will need to consider your approach even more carefully.

The meeting itself can be quite a pleasant affair if you have two people in the right frame of mind and the agenda itself is framed in the right way. Personal style can have a big impact, bearing in mind that you are being critical of other department's behaviour, performance or style.

I recommend setting the scene at the outset, explaining what your team has been doing, the purpose of the meeting and what you hope to get out of it. I often approach these types of conversation in a very humble manner, explaining that I am here to find ways that our team can work more effectively with the other person's team. The approach, of course, will depend on who you are and who you are dealing with. The general approach of trying to learn what is the reality of the situation and what needs to happen, rather than being accusatory from the outset, invariably works better.

Once you have discovered their point of view, identified what needs further investigation and what needs to be addressed immediately you can then form your action plans.

Step 7 – (Collaborative) mini projects.

The actions from the previous step's meetings form the basis of your mini projects. Many projects will be collaborative in nature as other departments may need to learn more about how your department works in order to create optimal solutions that improve the situation for both departments.

It can be worth splitting the projects into two groups. There will most likely be a number of 'quick wins' to consider, short projects that will yield immediate results. There will also be a number of longer term projects that will need to be considered and scheduled. It is important that momentum is not lost from the earlier team exercise and so performing the quick wins immediately is a good strategy.

If you are trying to figure out where to start in terms of organising your projects then consider the projects that are with the high transaction departments. It is probable that you will have relationships with a number of departments, but a couple of them will be higher volume in nature. These higher volume partnerships are where the biggest gains are likely to be made and I recommend that you consider these first. The more you can leverage your improvement projects the better the effect will be for your department and the business overall.

MRP systems are joined up by design. You need to make sure that your teams are joined up too.

Action Step:

- Follow the above steps if your internal teams do not link up as you need them to in order to run your MRP system effectively.

Links With Lean

In many circles Lean and MRP are seen as philosophically opposed. With a degree of creativity it is possible to use the best bits of both systems to drive efficiency and control within your business. Although this subject could (again) be a book in its own right, I will cover the key aspects of running both systems in parallel when it comes to production scheduling.

For those of you who are not familiar with Lean it strives to eliminate waste from the business and can lead you into a 'pull' production system. MRP is based on meeting a timetable of production, and hence is referred to as a 'push' production system. The seven wastes that Lean refers to are primarily defects, overproduction, transport, waiting, inventory, motions and processing. If I take each waste in turn you will be able to see how the two approaches do in fact have common goals.

Defects are not wanted by either system. Defects need to be driven out by better operator engagements and through better processing equipment, methods and design. Erroneous data in your MRP system can lead to defects.

Overproduction is not wanted by either system. The supply and demand equation in MRP aims to leave a system with zero stock. A kanban (visual signal) pull production system aims to minimise stock in the process too. A kanban can take many forms. It may be a space on the floor that indicates production is to proceed when the square is empty, or it may be a card system that indicates the downstream departments require more work.

Transportation is a common goal of both MRP and Lean. Minimising the cost of production by avoiding having to move it is an objective for any business.

Waiting is the first waste that actually shows a difference in approach. MRP will schedule production based on the rules that you give to it. If you have a five week period for scheduling and the work content is only eight hours then those eight hours could be evenly spread through the five weeks. They could also be tightly bunched at the start or end of the same period. Pull production systems are designed to produce the work at the latest possible time and perform all the operations in one seamless run. The on time delivery performance can be the same, but the way to get there can be completely different. You can often achieve a shorter lead time (and reduce delays) by shortening the overall production period, but delays will still be present.

Inventory is also driven to achieve zero stock in both systems. Both Lean and modern day MRP based supply chain management approaches look to develop supplier relationships that can make replenishing stock more responsive, leading to lower stock holding requirements. MRP will always try to balance supply and demand, leading to zero stock. Lean aims to do the same. However, if your MRP system has details for safety stock, and other stocking requirements, then MRP will execute your instructions and suggest that you need to hold stock.

Motions are a waste that is focussed on in Lean. MRP doesn't directly refer to motions, but it is another aspect of good management / engineering that can be executed that doesn't diverge from MRP's principles.

Processes need to be slick whether in MRP or Lean. The previous section in particular and other sections throughout this book look to improve the supporting processes of MRP. Lean looks to find those processes that don't work either efficiently or effectively and re-engineer them. Both approaches try to do the same thing. Lean however can be applied more readily to shop floor activities, where significant gains can be made.

Lean can be summarised as driving out waste from a business' operation in order to maximise the value adding operations. This should be a goal for any business, whether you call it Lean or anything else. There is a lot of synergy between Lean and MRP, but the fundamental difference as I see it is the shop floor scheduling approach. An immediate criticism of the Lean approach is its perceived inflexibility. Many people believe a pull production system will only work if you have a limited range of products to produce. This isn't true of course, but when you see car factories on the TV you can understand where the myth comes from. I have worked in the automotive sector and we merged pull and push production systems successfully. I have also worked with bespoke engineered products and used pull systems effectively. If you are prepared to be flexible then you can use the strengths of the different systems to complement each other.

If you have complexity in your order books and / or your Bills of Materials then MRP lends itself for the re-ordering process. It is a tried and tested system and if you configure the stock settings you can minimise the stock holdings. MRP is an effective database approach to inventory management and can help you to keep the necessary controls in place. Various kanbans can be used to re-order materials, but it is up to you how much control you want over stock levels. Kanbans for small low cost components (such as fasteners, clips and covers) can work well, but if you are managing castings etc. specific order requests via MRP may be more appropriate.

Pull production for the works orders can be a beautiful sight to behold. When you have spent the time designing the production lines, replenishment systems and breaking the product down into packets of work it can be breath taking to see the autonomous coordination of a pull production system. No expediters chasing parts, no Production Managers shouting to get orders moving, pure production excellence. It can take a long time to get a business this organised to move into pull production. If you follow the Lean model put forward by Womack and Jones there are three stages prior to pull. You have the Value recognition stage (what will your clients give you money for) followed by the Value Stream stage (how you create value). The next stage is called Flow (eliminating waste primarily) and then you move to Pull (demand driven production). The final stage is termed Perfection and embodies the art and science of continuous improvement. Jumping to Pull without doing the groundwork leads to disaster, which I have witnessed many businesses do. Pull is sexy (relatively, in manufacturing terms); hard work to get you there is not.

As I have said several times already, being flexible with the principles is the key to a good implementation. Whatever you do to implement a pull production system there is one obstacle that you need to consider – packet sizes. Most kanban driven systems request specific parts; hence the belief that pull production is for low variety businesses. You can ignore the part and instead focus on the production request solely. If you can find a way to break down your workloads into even packet sizes (by grouping / breaking up operations, or calculating batch sizes) then you can introduce a pull production system. Balance is the key here. Lean production systems aim for 'single piece flow', but this may be difficult to achieve based on setup times and variety of parts. SMED (Single Minute Exchange of Dies) is a method to reduce setup times so that you can become more flexible in your production plans. Even with this kind of investment in time you may find that you still aren't able to handle a pull production system. Cell creation to handle similar types of work may take you a step closer. Flowing similar work down specific production 'lines' can help you to package the work more effectively and therefore should be considered if it can help you to become more efficient in your production of the parts.

You might be asking yourself at this point 'what tells the Lean production system, or kanbans, what orders to work on?' This is one of the primary links with MRP. The capacity planning, and contract review process, can still remain as they are. The work to list is now only used at the workcentres / cells that initiate production. Work is consumed through a pull system in a 'first in first out' (FIFO) way, so flow around the business accordingly. Again you can see the work required to make sure it is obvious how work must flow around your business.

The ideas associated with Lean can be applied into your office practices as well, and I recommend that you don't stop on the shop floor. Many times it is the office that is hiding delays and lead time bloating activities.

Lean can be used in conjunction with MRP with no side effects. The degree to which you want to pursue Lean and a pull production system is your choice. There is a lot of work to do in order to create an environment where this is possible. If you have some degree of stability in your product mix (forgetting variety), or the flexibility to package work then a pull system could be worth investing in. If your business however deals in one offs and low volume high variety products it may be more worthwhile to optimise your MRP system and use Lean to streamline every supporting process.

Lean is a big subject nowadays and certainly worthy of further reading and investigation.

Action Steps:

- Identify your product streams / production methods and get a feel for whether a Lean production system can be integrated with your MRP system.

- Streamline your supporting processes by identifying the wastes in the process and eliminating them accordingly.

- Optimise your MRP system to reduce stock holding.

- Identify the strengths of each approach to develop your optimal approach.

- Consider using MRP to control the flow of work into your business and then using the lean pull systems to manage the subsequent work streams.

- Read up on Lean if you haven't got prior experience. There is a lot of preparatory work to do in order to merge MRP systems with Lean production schedules.

The Report Writing Trap

Report writers are an incredibly useful aid to running and managing MRP systems. The ability to draw out information so that you can use it to make swift and accurate decisions is invaluable. On the flip side of this there is the issue that not managing the requests and back catalogue of reports can cause an administrative headache further down the line.

When designing reports it is best to work from a specification. What does the person who asked for the report really want? Report writing can be a lot faster process when you know what you are trying to do. The first trap to avoid is not having a specification supplied when writing a report.

A real crime from a report writing perspective is people not using the reports once they are created. If the report is useful in nature then it needs to find a way into your routines. The second trap is not using the reports you already have.

When a new MRP system is introduced there can often be an explosion of reports. Keeping this under control can be a real challenge. Referring back to the previous point, if the specification is supplied then it can be reviewed. It is also highly likely that there are only a handful of people within your business who will be capable of writing reports. By allowing requests to write reports into their queues in batches (let's say weekly batches) it becomes easier to spot duplication. I have seen many reports being written, by very accommodating people, which fundamentally do the same thing as earlier reports. Training your report writing staff to challenge similar or duplicate reports is a useful tactic. So, the third trap is the duplication and explosion of reports being created.

To extend the idea of preventing duplication of both reports and effort how about creating a report log? If you create a log, such as in a spreadsheet program, you can help to manage and maintain your repository of reports. Aside from the duplication there is the issue that if people don't understand what reports are available to them then they won't use them. Writing reports only becomes a useful activity if the tools get used for productive action. The log doesn't need to be complicated; the following headings are a good place to start:

- Department
- Report name
- Purpose of report
- Filename and location
- Revision

A well maintained log can help to prevent duplicated effort and keep your computer files tidier by having less of them.

If your business has already created a vast array of reports to date then rationalising what you already have makes sense. If you don't have a report log then creating one will help you to identify what each report does and whether its functionality is duplicating that of another report. Once you have found out what all of your reports do there are two questions to ask:

1 – Can I delete the duplicate / redundant reports (and which one do I keep)?

2 – What functionality is the business missing, what reports should I request?

It can take a little bit of time and a number of people to go through this process but having a tidier collection of reports that actually get used (because the fog has lifted and the reports are now accessible) is worth the effort. A well designed report can save you many hours of work in order to make important decisions. I urge you to both embrace the report writer and to keep the creation of reports under control.

Action Steps:

- Create a report log that allows system users to quickly identify the reports that they need.

- Remove duplicate reports.

- Add in missing reports.

- Build key reports into your routines.

Summary

In this section I have looked at a number of areas that can help you to make the management of your MRP system even more effective and productive.

Using automation and exception reporting can really decrease the amount of time needed to properly manage the operation. Effective report writing is part of this equation.

Ensuring that the correct privileges are in place for system access, combined with a simple auditing process can help to make sure that the right activities are being undertaken by the right people at the right time.

Collaborating with other departments to better understand the interactions and relationships can allow you to develop improvement plans that can deliver tangible benefits.

And, by touching upon the links with Lean, I hope you see that this mature software approach could still have a place in your business should you be striving to move down the Lean route when it comes to business improvement.

In our final section I will share with you some of my thoughts on how to manage improvement projects and continuous improvement activities. The intention is that you can pull the ideas in this book together for your business' benefit in a practical way.

Section Five - Action Planning

Now it is time to put the ideas you have gained from reading this book into action. I want you to be able to move past 'having a nice read' to 'seeing the results'.

This final section of the book will share some ideas on how to collate and design your improvement plans. I will also share some of my thoughts on how continuous improvement fails in many businesses and how you can apply these insights to your own business. I should also state that these pages aren't just for MRP systems; the same approach can be used for other areas of your business.

As you have gone through this book I hope that you have identified specific areas of your system that you want to improve. Many improvements opportunities will be obvious based on how this book is split up. For example, if your Bills of Materials are inadequate then creating a plan to fix them is a logical next step. Also, if you realise that you are missing disciplines about how you work day to day then that is a clear area for you to focus on. By the time you have reviewed where you are you may well find that you have quite a number of improvements to make.

Having numerous short plans is not a bad thing. I recommend to my clients that they use small projects to help motivate staff to complete the improvements. Having many smaller victories can help your team to keep going and can make getting them started easier. In most cases when people see a large project they can become nervous about the size of the challenge and procrastination can result. Smaller projects help to put people at ease and when sequenced properly can be a remedy to stalling improvements.

The key to using smaller plans is to ensure that they link together and are coordinated. Many small plans can link to one main part of the system. Prioritise these plans and use the sequence to manage the activity. By coordinating all of the elements, whether through a weekly update meeting, or through a single person, you will be able to make swift progress.

The rest of this section of the book will look at how we create our plans, manage the priorities, manage implementation and develop a continuous improvement approach that works.

Elements Of Your Plan

From reading this book you should have identified at least some part of your plan. The most obvious items to include in your list are the 'corrective actions' that you need to undertake. If there are several steps to complete these actions, such as making decisions, planning the resources etc. then include these into your plan.

Prioritising a number of quick wins is a good approach to take when organising your plans. Getting a few victories is helpful to build confidence and momentum in your business to complete the future plans. Some of these will be single actions that you can perform, so where possible don't let them get lost in later phases of your plan.

The collaborative projects will need to be developed in conjunction with the other departments. Their views and their actions will need to built up into a joint plan. Don't forget to include them or momentum can really be lost!

So all of this may seem pretty obvious, but what about the times when you are not sure what to put into your plan? A simple approach called 'B to A' planning can help us here.

B to A simply means that instead of starting where we are and developing a plan of action, we start at the end and work backwards. If you have never done this before then it can seem to be a strange approach. With a little practice you should be able to do this swiftly and create more direct plans than before. B to A gives you a direct route from your goal back to where you are. A to B planning (or the more traditional route) can lead you down different paths that may not be the most direct.

To plan using the B to A method place yourself mentally at your outcome. For example, perhaps your goal is to have 98% plus on time delivery performance, above target profit margins and a growing customer base. Starting from this point, what was the last thing you did? You will have to imagine what the last step before this point was and the answer will be different for everyone. The point of doing this exercise is to get our brains going and develop options for our plans. You may answer, for this particular example, that the last thing before this point was winning an award from one of your major customers in terms of delivery performance. Before that you may imagine:

- congratulating your teams for the improvements they have made.

- allowing the team to create their own plans for making the necessary changes.

- setting up the teams that were going to make the changes.

- specifying specific performance objectives and outlining the changes required.

- analysing the information from the key focal areas.

- identifying the key areas that need improvement.

- fixing the basic errors in the MRP system.

- reviewing the report on the errors in the MRP system.

- requesting the reports for the BoMs, routings and shop floor booking accuracy.

- meeting with your team to review where the business is in terms of performance.

I hope this example shows you how you can imagine your way back to the present day. The idea is that you end up with the straightest line possible. To help you to validate this approach you may also want to consider what immediate steps you can see now before you and how they fit in with your B to A plan. Having a few minutes break from the plan and returning to it can let you see gaps in your previous thinking. It can take practice to use this method, but it can certainly help your planning when you get stuck and can't see the way forward. I know some of my clients use a combination of B to A and A to B planning to try and find their optimum approach. Try it and see what plans you generate.

As an outcome for your plans it is helpful to identify how you build your new processes into your ongoing management. Find opportunities to build checks and balances into your regular management meetings. Using, or creating, process based Key Performance Indicators (KPIs) can help you keep a handle on the new ways of working that come out from your plans and ultimately help you to continue to improve your business systems and processes.

For each element of your plan it is worth identifying:

- Who is going to deliver the element.

- How they are going to deliver it.

- When they are going to deliver it.

- How much time they need.

- The risk of this person being in charge (i.e. do you need to check up with them before the deadline?)

A fully formed plan is a wonderful thing. Execution without a good plan is usually chaos and time invested in planning is well worth it.

Action Steps:

- Identify the quick win actions you can take immediately.

- Use B to A planning if you cannot see the route to take when developing your project plan.

- Consider the usual variables of who, what, when and how when developing your plan.

- Put in the necessary checks during the project activity to make sure that your team are going to be able to hit their deadlines. The frequency of checks and their necessity will depend upon the experience and reliability of the person performing the task.

Prioritisation Of Plans

I have already mentioned quick wins and their need for early implementation. One point that I want to touch on is a simple way to work out what goes first in your overall sequence of plans.

A great project to plan for could be one that:

- Has a massive positive impact for the business.

- Costs very little to implement.

- Can be implemented quickly and easily.

You can develop your own criteria and include any factors that you want to. Some businesses that use this approach use it as a group decision tool to move projects up and down the order of execution. Others create grading systems where specific impacts have specific scores associated with them. They do the same for cost and speed / ease of implementation. By multiplying the three scores you end up with a total score. This final score can then be ranked and a (more) objective sequence derived.

I see many businesses who chase around working on projects without ever stopping to consider what would give them the 'biggest bang for their buck'. Don't fall into this trap of letting your teams become busy fools.

Action Steps:

- Create a scoring system that makes sense to your business and gives you the best return for your efforts.

- Score your improvement projects and set to work on the 'top priority' project.

- Periodically review the list as new projects may have been added to the list. Re-score as appropriate and establish the new priority order.

Follow Through

If you have studied Lean in more depth, or have used quality management systems (such as ISO 9001) then you will know about PDCA.

At the heart of these systems PDCA helps to control and measure improvements to a business' performance. PDCA is also known as the 'Deming Cycle' or 'Continuous Improvement Cycle' and stands for:

- Plan

- Do

- Check

- Act

Planning and doing seems to come naturally to a lot of businesses, but checking and acting does not. Have you seen perfectly good ideas assigned to the bin because they didn't work the first time? I've seen too many.

When an improvement has arrived at a logical point to be reviewed this is your opportunity to ask 'did it achieve the desired results?' Based on the answer you can:

- be happy with what happened and close out the improvement

- be unhappy, work out how big the gap is between actual and desired results, decide what you have learned and then design a second approach

Of course, sometimes you will decide not to invest any more time and effort in an improvement, but I suggest that this is done from a position of information. Just knowing that the result wasn't achieved is not enough. Knowing how far away you were and what you have learned is central to establishing what you should do next. Real learning takes place here and that is how you can make your business become better and better. I have seen many improvements fall over to find out much later that a small tweak in approach, education, mathematics, or something else is all that it actually took to make it work. Don't fall foul of the next tiny step that can make all of the difference.

I touched upon the close out of an improvement above. By this I mean that the A in PDCA implies that we act accordingly with the information we found at the check stage. If you are going to go through the cycle again then it may be preparing for the next planning session. If you are happy with the result then it may be developing the appropriate Standard Operating Procedures (SOPs), memo or other communications that will help put the new practices in place.

PDCA is both a simple and powerful approach. Using it in conjunction with your improvement plans can give you a real boost in keeping your teams onboard with the change process as well as helping to ensure that more of your improvement ideas get implemented. At the end of the day it is the results that count and you need to make sure that your improvement plans come to fruition. Don't miss out the C and A of PDCA!

Action Steps:

- Determine what the appropriate 'close out' methods are for your business when delivering improvement projects.
- Adhere to the PDCA cycle when implementing changes to control the process.

Bite Size Chunks

In the introduction to this section I wrote about using smaller project plans to help your team to engage with the change process. Commonly this approach is referred to as 'Kaizen', but often this word is misunderstood. Tiny steps can work wonders when improvement activity is stalling, and this approach is not just for generating small improvement ideas, it is central to the initiation of continuous improvement activity.

When people are faced with big tasks this has the potential to 'freak them out' and cause delays with implementing change. Big is a very subjective word. What is big to you might be tiny, or massive, to me. The only agreeable size is when we get down to really small elements of work. When these small chunks of work get so small usually everyone can agree that the work involved is small and so this is one place we can go to gain agreement.

When we take the tiny steps approach we are attempting to circumnavigate the 'fight or flight' response. Whereas in the wild this reaction may be stimulated by an approaching lion, in our place of work this can be triggered by an increasing workload / moving out of our comfort zone. For this reason the response could be restated as the 'execute or procrastinate' response. Procrastination is what usually happens when the task seems too large or too complicated to proceed with.

When your team takes a small nibble of a project that they previously haven't attempted they start to gain feedback. They gain confidence and grow as individuals. Their ability to perform increases, as does their ability to take bigger and bigger steps towards completing improvement projects. What once was big now seems OK to them. For those of you thinking that the tiny steps approach will take forever there are two responses. Firstly, slow progress is often better than no progress. Secondly, that isn't what usually happens. A slow start often accumulates into much faster progress than you would normally experience. As confidence grows you can start to observe improvement projects being handled much faster and more competently than before.

If your projects are stalled, or not starting, then using this approach can work wonders. Take the first few items from the project and break them down so that they are really small. Let your team get to grips with the project on their own terms and let them grow into delivering the project. It can take a degree of trust to use this approach, but I haven't seen a business yet that hasn't made this approach work.

Action Steps:

- Identify which improvement projects are stalling.

- Break the first few steps down into really small steps.

- Let your team progress with these actions at their own rate.

- Support your team through the entire process.

- Observe their development; are they able to take on bigger and bigger challenges?

Continuous Improvement

After your first set of improvement activities you will hopefully be in a position where your performance has improved and your MRP system is working well. Where do you go from here? Continuous improvement is a much used term and one that I find rarely makes it from being sporadic to continuous. There is also the challenge that once a business gets past its initial problems the activity dries up. Moving from good to excellent is a different conversation than moving from bad to ok. When things are bad they are easy to spot. You know what isn't working and you want to fix the situation. When the issues aren't as visible (because everything is working ok) spotting the opportunities can be harder. When it gets harder this is the point that improvement activities slow down, for obvious reasons.

Generating ideas to improve a business takes imagination. Imagining what the business processes could be in the future, what would be an amazing future state is something that for many takes practice. Giving your team the opportunity to exercise their imaginations on a regular basis is certainly a challenge for any leader but can be done with some simple approaches. Here are two for example:

- Break down your business into its processes and for each process consider one performance criteria. For example, how do you make your <u>invoicing</u> operate <u>faster</u>? By putting your business into small compartments, with context, it can be a lot easier for your team to generate ideas. Other performance criteria could include making the process simpler, more robust, cheaper etc...

- Using a role model can be useful to reflect upon and generate options for improvement. Think of a company that you admire. If they had your business processes what would they do? How would they approach improving it to bring it in line with their other ways of working? Using their perspective can help you to identify new opportunities.

Keep working on projects that will yield the greatest value for your business. Use your KPIs to gauge progress and tell you objectively what impact you are having on your business. When you can explain your improvement activities in objective terms to your superiors then conversations usually run more smoothly.

The biggest challenge of any continuous improvement is how to move away from solely project orientated activity to inspired action at all levels of the business. In my experience using the formal group activity to grow and expand participation can lead to this organic activity taking place throughout the business. Defining what sort of project needs to be in a weekly improvement meeting (for example) and what can be trialled and tested without going via the meeting is a good way to provide clarity. If people think that everything has to go through the meeting you may find that some people are uncomfortable with declaring their ideas in a public setting. Allowing them a degree of freedom can help to build confidence and they can then come back to the group with their findings / results. In our MRP context, this may be a case of playing with part of the demo system and coming back to the group with their results from the testing. Mentoring specific team members to nurture their ideas is a good option too. There is always a range of ability and enthusiasm when it comes to generating and undertaking improvement activity. Those who you find to be interested are prime candidates for mentoring and support. Their colleagues who are 'on the fence' regarding improvements can then witness their peers making improvements and this could influence their engagement.

This approach can take time, once you get another staff member generating, testing and implementing their own ideas it can be like hitting a thick vein of gold. I have experienced it personally when even just a few members of one of my teams started producing (or revealing) their own ideas. With a modest amount of support and guidance some of their ideas revolutionised the production flow through their departments (and increased flexibility and capacity). It was brilliant to watch and worth the effort. In Lean the eighth waste is 'untapped human potential' (an addition to the seven wastes we discussed briefly in the last section). The knowledge, experiences, observations and insights in our team are sitting there. It is your job as a leader to help bring out and facilitate these ideas so that your business can improve.

Don't forget PDCA and close out your ongoing improvements in the most appropriate fashion.

Action Steps:

- Identify some role models you can use to reflect upon to generate improvement ideas.
- Write a list of your processes and a list of performance areas. Use these in combination to provide your team a narrow focus to generate improvement ideas.
- Clarify what kind of improvement testing can be done without prior approval and what can't.
- Support a handful of people to experiment and test their ideas. Encourage the identification and implementation of improvement ideas to flow without you having to constantly drive the changes.

Summary

From this final section of the book I wanted you to get a feel for how you can take your own improvements past the ideas contained in this book. It is vital for any business to be able to identify both their 'hotspots' for improvement as well as generating ideas for non problem areas. Once the main problems you are facing have been dealt with becoming more creative and experimental is the real mark of continuous improvement that is working.

How you plan out your improvement projects can make a big difference to their ease of implementation. Using the B to A method, or whatever works for you, can make breaking down a plan into palatable bite size chunks easier. Prioritisation can be made straightforward by determining your criteria for evaluation in advance. Starting with 'quick wins' that are easy to implement and have a big impact can provide confidence and momentum for your team. Carrying on this approach into the remaining projects will serve you well.

The follow up is vital; ensuring good ideas are fully explored before being classed as unworkable for your business. The C in PDCA should become your friend. Find out how close your improvement was, correct if necessary, and then go again. It is rare that we find an improvement works perfectly the first time, exactly the way we want it. This opportunity for learning should be embraced to allow for bigger and better improvements to flow from the original attempt. From this perspective you can look at continuous improvement being more focussed on small trials and pilots than grand change programmes. Combining the Kaizen / tiny steps approach with PDCA gives you a low risk method for trying out ideas, and some will be spectacular.

Conclusion

Here we are, at the end of our time together looking at MRP and its surrounding topics.

If you:

- approach your MRP system correctly and choose how you want it to work,

- set up the key elements of your MRP system to reflect your reality of working,

- use and manage the system with discipline and routine,

- develop your system over time to take advantage of the learning and insight you have available in your business,

then you have a recipe for operating a slick MRP system.

These types of system have been around for over fifty years and it is time that more businesses got them working properly. No longer should you be the slave to these systems, it is time that you got in the driving seat and made them take you to where you want to go. Your business plans can be executed via MRP, if it is the right approach for your business. No longer shall workarounds and poorly configured systems rule the working day.

Work through the sections of this book again and identify the parts of this book that resonate with you. Fix the parts that make sense and check your results. Sections four and five are more focussed on moving past the problems and getting into your own improvement experiments. Start small if you are concerned about the effect of your experiments and use your demo system to prove out your ideas. Figure out how your system thinks and then decide how best to manage and manipulate your system.

Let your system take the strain and get on with adding the true value that humans can add; creativity, relationship building and innovation.

Thank you for reading this book. I have spent the last fifteen years of my working life involved with MRP systems. I love Lean, but sometimes the sheer number crunching ability of MRP is what is required. Find the ideal fit for your business and go to work.

I wish you every success with making your MRP system work the way you had hoped for.

Giles

Links and Resources

Smartspeed Blog

For more ideas on how to improve your business and to find out how to apply some of the more common business improvement ideas in novel ways please visit our blog:

www.smartspeed.info

Free On Time Delivery Report

If you want some ideas around improving the on time delivery performance of your business, then please download our free report. You will need to register your email address on our website, the link is:

www.systemsandprocesses.co.uk

LinkedIn OTIF Forum

If you would like to join us online to discuss practical ideas around improving on time delivery performance then please visit our LinkedIn group:

http://www.linkedin.com/groups/On-Time-Delivery-Improvement-4419220/about

About Giles Johnston

Giles is a Chartered Engineer with a background in Operations Management who spends most of his time working on capacity planning and 'on time delivery' improvement projects.

He has worked in a variety of different roles within manufacturing prior to working as a consultant for a prestigious university.

In 2005 Giles decided to forge his own path and created Smartspeed, which has been helping businesses to improve their delivery performance, along with their profits, ever since.

Giles can be contacted by:

Email -   **gilesjohnston@smartspeed.co.uk**

Website -   **www.smartspeed.co.uk**

Smartspeed's Contact Details

Thank you for purchasing this book, if you have any comments we would love to read them.

www.smartspeed.co.uk

(t) +44 191 645 3086

(e) **info@smartspeed.co.uk**

For information about our other products and consulting services please get in touch using the details above.

Printed in Great
Britain
by Amazon